Cash in the attic

Paul Hayes

BBC BOOKS

This book is published to accompany the television series *Cash in the Attic*, produced for BBC Television by Leopard Films.

Series Producer: Bernard Periatambee
Executive Producer: James Burstall
Commissioning Executive for the BBC: Dominic Vallely

Published by BBC Books, BBC Worldwide Ltd,
Woodlands, 80 Wood Lane, London W12 0TT

First published 2004

ISBN 0 563 48791 7

Commissioning Editor: Vivien Bowler
Project Editor: Christopher Tinker
Copy-editor: Judith Scott
Art Director: Sarah Ponder
Design: Grade Design Consultants
Picture Researcher: Victoria Hall

Set in Helvetica Neue and OCRB
Printed and bound in France by Imprimerie Pollina s.a. - N° L92705
Colour separations by Radstock Reproductions Ltd., Midsomer Norton, England

BBC Worldwide would like to thank the following for providing photographs and permission to reproduce copyright material. While every effort has been made to trace and acknowledge all copyright holders, we would like to apologize should there have been any errors or omissions.

All images BBC *Homes & Antiques* magazine/Clive Cordless apart from the following: Alamy/JanineWiedel Photolibrary 128; BBC/Gary Moyes 2, 6, 10; BBC *Homes & Antiques* magazine/Andrew Montgomery 33, 41; BBC *Homes & Antiques* magazine/Steve Dalton 56, 70; Christies Images 16, 26, 126; © John Clarke 144; Corbis Sygma/Maurice Rougemont 12; Corbis/Tim Graham 100; Corbis Sygma/Jacques Langevin 133; Narratives/Jan Baldwin 20, 48, 120; Narratives/Tamsyn Hill 58; Narratives/Richard Jessop 72; Narratives/Josephine Ryan 38; Rex Features/Nils Jorgensen 111.

Page 2: Jonty Hearnden, Alistair Appleton and Paul Hayes – the *Cash in the Attic* team.

If you love beautiful things in your home, then Homes & Antiques *is the magazine to enjoy receiving each month. Its unique blend of classic and contemporary looks makes it the magazine for today's stylish homemaker. Add to this inspiring features on the arts, antiques, gardening and travel and you have a magazine to satisfy every aspiration. There is only one* Homes & Antiques. *Call 0870 444 7011 quoting ATTIC04 to subscribe.*

Cash in the attic

Contents

Foreword

Who collects? Well, if my ad-hoc research in the field is credible, then everyone does. I've just come back from filming *Cash in the Attic* in Barrow-in-Furness, where, over bacon and eggs in the hotel, a dockworker in his fifties was saying how much he enjoyed the show. A week earlier, at the Notting Hill Carnival, a gang of 16-year-old students waylaid me with enthusiasm for all things antique.

But as I travel up and down the UK, sipping tea in people's kitchens, admiring their multifarious collections and – more importantly – hearing the stories behind their collecting urges, I've often asked myself: why do people collect? What drives a 60-year-old bachelor to live with over 10,000 books? Or an ex-prison warder to have 300 carved elephants and the same number of painted thimbles? What makes a former drayman pay £150 for a Beatrix Potter figurine or an 80-year-old pensioner travel the country looking for irons?

Well, firstly, there's a deep-seated predilection in human beings for putting like with like. Our Stone Age forebears probably stumbled across one mammoth's tooth and then decided two looked rather nice together. Then before they knew it – kapow! – 12 dozen mammoths' teeth all lined up in a display cabinet and categorized according to size and dental detail.

That urge to arrange and amass informs everything from teenage stamp collections to Victorian lepidoptery. It's probably what drove one of our contributors, a charming dentist from Sheffield, to become the country's biggest collector of moustache cups. But alongside that there's a simpler desire to feather our nest with things – beautiful things, preferably, but also valuable things, things that were hard to find and things that are loaded with memories from loved ones who've passed away.

This is certainly one of the most interesting aspects of *Cash in the Attic* for me. I've often been swept away as a certain object releases a torrent of emotion in someone we're filming. There was a powerful example of this in our first series, when we met a couple whose young son, also a collector, had died. When they were clearing out his possessions they found a docket from the repair shop for his last purchase, a mantel clock, which they brought back and sat on their mantelpiece. The ticking heartbeat of their departed son. These sorts of items are beyond value.

But there are many inherited items that leave us feeling more ambivalent. Stuff we've acquired through the deaths of parents or grandparents naturally has some sentimental value but in many cases there's too much of it and all these things – Grandma's sideboard, Aunt Myrtle's tea set, Uncle Roy's Airfix models – become burdensome.

Our own collecting can become a burden too. Sometimes we grow out of a passion and are reluctant to let go of it. For example, we've come across many houses on the show that are weighed down by heavy mahogany furniture long after the owner's passion for Victoriana has passed.

In fact, many of the homes we visit show symptoms of severe clutteritis: guest rooms groaning under junk boxes and broken china, dining rooms impossible to dine in because of the 19 almost complete teasets, attics filled to bursting with all the children's school exercise books going back to 1967.

So the problem is this: where does collection end and clutter begin? Essentially it's a question of value. If the things you own are worth something – that is if they're in good condition, of high quality and sought after on today's market – then they're worth collecting. If they're broken, shabby, cheaply made or impossibly out of date then they're junk. And too much junk can choke your home.

Which is where Paul's amazingly useful guide to valuation, buying and selling comes in. It's a life-saver for two separate groups. Firstly, for those chronic collectors whose passions have filled their houses to the brim and who no longer know what to keep and what to bin. Knowing your porcelain from your pottery and your spelter from your silver means you can sift the pearls of your collection from the rubbish. Secondly, for beginners. If you're just starting sniffing around auction houses and car boots, you can make informed decisions about what you want to collect in the first place. With this book in your possession you'll soon be filling your nest with beautiful, valuable and worthwhile feathers rather than broken twigs and worthless bric-a-brac.

In the world of collectables, knowledge is power. Know what you've got, keep what's worth it and offload the rest. Then at least you'll know what the select pieces you have are worth so if further down the line you need to release some assets you'll have a good idea of what they'll bring at auction.

Which brings us to the most exciting part of the antiques world: the auction room. Before I started filming *Cash* I'd never been to an auction and certainly never thought about buying anything there. Now I would never dream of buying new furniture, for example, without visiting local auction houses first. For one, you can pick up incredible bargains at auctions (and not just at your classic saleroom, I'm including car boots and internet auction sites here as well). And secondly, it's a unique thrill, lifting up your little bidder's paddle and bidding on an item or – more profitably – watching other people bid like crazy for Aunt Myrtle's tea set. If you've not been to an auction to bid or to sell, then rectify that error immediately and get down to your local saleroom.

But don't on any account go without having read and memorized Mr Hayes' advice in the following pages. With more than 20 years' experience in the trade, he knows everything there is to know about getting a bargain and, more importantly, not getting ripped off. So read the book, sort out your attic and when you've finished, get selling …

Alistair Appleton, presenter of *Cash in the Attic*

Introduction

I was invited to write this book as a guide for those who, like the people appearing on the BBC's *Cash in the Attic* programme, might wish to dispose of things that are taking up space and are no longer wanted in the home. The fact is that almost anything old (I won't attempt to define the word 'antique' just yet) will appeal to somebody somewhere and with my knowledge of the antiques trade I can help you get the best prices for your valuables.

So do you need to raise some money for a special purpose? Then set yourself a target sum and take a good look at what you have around the house. It may look like a load of old junk at the moment but don't be in too much of a hurry to throw it out. Use this book to identify what you have and to work out what it might be worth.

A word of warning before you start, though. I have loved antiques and collectables since I was a schoolboy. I was brought up in the trade and I cannot remember a time when I was not fascinated by the glimpse into our history that so many of these old objects afford. For me this is a passion and perhaps there is a slight risk that some of this enthusiasm will rub off on you. Far from rushing to get rid of your treasures, you could find yourself wanting to learn more about them. Even worse, you might decide to hold on to them after all – and then you might just be tempted to go out and buy some more to add to your collection.

If that happens, I have to confess that I will not be sorry – but please don't tell the BBC!

Paul Hayes

1

Getting started

Once you have made the decision to sell your unwanted items, it's a good idea to sort everything into categories and make a list. If you have enough space, collect everything together in one place. When you have done this, you are ready to start your research. You will only be able to come up with a reasonable estimate of how much something is likely to be worth if you know exactly what it is and, if possible, when and where it was made. Visible wear or damage won't necessarily make an item unsaleable but it will probably lower the value, so make a note of the general condition of each piece.

Is it a genuine antique?

It is generally accepted within the trade that an antique is any object that is more than a hundred years old. This definition is also used in law and by Customs and Excise. People collect all sorts of things, of course, and just because something is not old enough to be a genuine antique doesn't mean that it will be worthless.

Think of a piece of pottery designed by Clarice Cliff in the 1930s, a bootleg Beatles recording from the 1960s or the very first Harry Potter novel, published in the 1990s. These items come under the general heading of 'collectables'. They become desirable and acquire a high resale value because the supply is limited and there are buyers all over the world competing with each other to pay good money for them. Popular collectables from the twentieth century include: pottery, jewellery, books (first editions), comics, cameras, photographs, postcards and showbiz memorabilia.

At the other end of the spectrum there are antiquities, which are artefacts surviving from ancient civilizations – Egyptian, Greek, Roman, etc., and all periods up to the end of the Middle Ages in the 1450s. Nowadays antiquities are likely to turn up wherever there are archaeological digs and most pieces end up in museums, though some find their way into private collections. The question of legal ownership, export and import regulations, and the buying and selling of antiquities (not to mention the huge number of fake objects in circulation) is fraught with difficulties and so they will not feature in this book.

After you have picked out the genuine antiques and worthwhile collectables you will be left with the real junk, fit only for a car boot sale, donation to a charity shop or jumble sale or, in the last resort, the dustbin. The most common items falling into this category are: electrical appliances, kitchen equipment and utensils, clothing, bedding and curtains, books, videos, records and CDs. Don't forget that in the UK it is illegal to sell second-hand electrical goods at a car boot sale – unless you remove the flex or cable first.

Rococo: a Chelsea vase made around 1765

Styles and periods

Every period in history has its own distinctive fashions and style and one of the aims of this book is to help you to recognize the typical features of design that characterize each age. After a while you will begin to see certain patterns emerging across the centuries that link the architecture with the art of a particular era right through to the smallest artefact.

And with a little bit of background knowledge you will be well on the way to being able to tell whether what you have in the attic is the real thing, a clever reproduction or just a poor substitute.

Rococo

This is a popular style associated with the Georgian era that emerged in the early 1700s and lasted for about a hundred years. It strikes many of us today as fussy and over-decorative, but when done well the effect can be stunning. Look for pastel colours and flamboyant embellishment, floral motifs and scrolls.

Neoclassicism

This style started in Rome in the middle of the eighteenth century, stimulated by the rediscovery of the lost cities of Pompeii and Herculaneum that were being excavated at this time. With its emphasis on the simple, classical forms of the ancient world, it was a stark contrast to the overblown Rococo style, and artists and architects from all over Europe responded enthusiastically. Elegant symmetry and proportion are the hallmarks of the Neoclassical style and common decorative motifs include Corinthian columns, figures in Greek or Roman dress, cherubs and acanthus leaves.

Empire style

Empire style is associated with Emperor Napoleon in France in the early 1800s. It can be seen as a branch of Neoclassicism with a touch of Egypt thrown in, this being due, no doubt, to Napoleon's earlier campaigns in North Africa. Typical features to look out for are gilding and ebonizing – and the ubiquitous sphinx's head.

Regency

While the Empire style was all the rage in France at the beginning of the nineteenth century, Britain was moving in a slightly different direction, coming up with the contemporaneous Regency style, which gets its name from the Prince Regent at the time (later George IV). This style, though still elegant, allowed a certain amount of embellishment.

The Arts and Crafts Movement

During the Industrial Revolution the machine was king and mass production brought hundreds of new and affordable items to the general population in Victorian Britain. The Arts and Crafts Movement, which emerged in the latter half of the nineteenth century, was a direct response to what designers like William Morris (see page 29) and the writer John

Neoclassical: a Sheraton settee

Ruskin saw as the ugliness of most of these factory products. They sought to return to the values of traditional craftsmanship in areas such as furniture-making, textiles, pottery and printing, using the techniques and natural materials, such as oak and pewter, from medieval times.

Art Nouveau

By about 1900 another movement had emerged that was sympathetic to the principles of Arts and Crafts and because it originally developed in Belgium and France it is still known by its French name – Art Nouveau. Artists and designers working with this 'new art' style drew their inspiration from nature but turned it into an erotic fantasy world, creating wondrously stylized flowers and exotic creatures. Lines were curved and swirling rather than straight and angular. The female form was idealized and exaggerated and women were typically represented as water nymphs, languid maidens with long flowing hair or vamps.

Art Deco

Art Deco pieces are instantly recognizable by their bold colours and clear-cut geometric shapes, inspired by the discovery in 1922 of Tutankhamen's tomb. It is a hard-edged and abstract style and it emerged in complete contrast to the somewhat dreamy romanticism of Art Nouveau. Art Deco finally dragged design into the modern world, celebrating new and exciting materials and banishing for ever the dark, heavy and over-elaborate styling of the Victorian and Edwardian age.

Art Nouveau: a Tiffany lamp

Thirty questions

Before you clear out the clutter, try this quiz to see how much you know about antiques. The answers are scattered throughout this book (or check page 141).

1. **What is bleeding?**
   a. when a dealer loses cash on a deal
   b. the running of one colour into another on some watercolours
   c. a term used when referred to silver plate that has worn away, leaving a reddish tinge

2. **What is a touch mark?**
   a. an impulsive bidder
   b. a mark found typically on tankards representing the manufacturer
   c. an accidental imprint on an oil painting

3. **What is spelter?**
   a. a zinc alloy used predominantly to mimic bronze
   b. an auctioneer's warm-up patter
   c. an alloy of lead and antimony

4. **What is foxing?**
   a. damage on the surface of a painting
   b. passing off a modern copy as an authentic antique
   c. a type of pattern most commonly found in silverware

5. **Who or what is Namgreb?**
   a. a Belgian variant of Delftware
   b. artwork looted during the Vietnam conflict
   c. a Viennese sculptor who signed his name backwards

6. **What is a 'dovetail'?**
   a. a method used to join two pieces of wood together
   b. a method of painting with a feather
   c. a name given to the spring movement in early clocks

7. **What is a chryselephantine?**
   a. a very large flower found as the centrepiece of some oriental porcelain
   b. a figure made from a combination of bronze and ivory
   c. a butterfly motif, usually made from enamel and used on brooches

8. **What is an Albert?**
   a. a portable Victorian reed organ
   b. a watch chain
   c. a jet setting in a mourning brooch

9. **What is a pontil mark?**
   a. the sharp lump left on hand-blown glassware
   b. an identifier on a communion vessel.
   c. the bridge emblem of the London hallmark

10. **What is a *tazza*?**
    a. a very shallow, flat dish with a short central stem
    b. a dodgy antique dealer (Australian slang)
    c. a decorated beer mug

11. What is tube lining?

a. the name given to a form of decoration used by many ceramic manufacturers.

b. a method of repairing broken china

c. the refreshments carried out to those riding to hounds, or the large silver plate used to carry this fare

12. What is *verre églomisé*?

a. a reverse painting on glass

b. a small glass bell used in some church services

c. an early viewfinder

13. What is a bezel?

a. a metal rim used to secure a piece of glass onto a clock or watch face

b. a sloping cut in glass

c. a jewel set into the handle of a sword

14. What is a chatelaine?

a. a platinum charm bracelet

b. a collection of items suspended from a chain

c. an item of French porcelain

15. The teddy bear got its name from whom?

a. King Edward VII

b. Edward Lear

c. Theodore Roosevelt

16. What is millefiore?

a. a heavy floral brocade

b. a painting technique

c. a floral design commonly used in paperweights

17. What is 'Bizarre'?

a. a range of Clarice Cliff pottery

b. a Catalan school of painting

c. an early board game

18. What is lost wax?

a. an early method of recording sound

b. a way of conserving precious documents

c. a process used to produce art glass

19. What does an anchor impressed into a silver drinking vessel indicate?

a. the Birmingham assay mark

b. a Royal Navy goblet (for the Loyal Toast to the Sovereign)

c. the highest grade of Sterling Silver

20. What is a demi hunter?

a. a gentleman's cane

b. an ornate cape

c. a partially encased pocket watch

21. What are affectionately known as Pip, Squeak and Wilfred?

a. a trio of medals

b. three famous London auction houses

c. the treble, mid-tone and bass horns of a clockwork gramophone

22. What is a 'Whimsie'?

a. a speculative bid at auction

b. the name given to miniature ceramic figurines made by the Staffordshire company Wade

c. an intentionally distorted copy of a porcelain figurine, usually unauthorized

23. What does NSA stand for?
a. New Scottish Academy
b. New Society of Artists
c. National Society of Architects

24. Where would you find tines?
a. on a pocket watch
b. around a coin
c. in a musical box

25. What is *Chinoiserie* a style of?
a. decorative or Fine Art
b. chinese embroidery
c. oriental sculpture

26. What is a 'stiffie'?
a. an item at auction that spectacularly fails to get near its expected price
b. a German pottery doll with articulated limbs
c. a piece of card that was used to make rigid a packet of cigarettes

27. What is a sampler?
a. a piece of needlework
b. a multi-compartment snuff box
c. a wine tasting glass

28. What is 'fusee'?
a. a clock movement
b. a means of soldering together two pieces of metal
c. a type of Chinese porcelain

29. Which ceramic company was originally best known for the manufacture of sewerage pipes?
a. Wade
b. Royal Doulton
c. Beswick

30. What is a carat?
a. a unit of weight
b. a unit of purity
c. a unit of volume

Turn to page 141 for the answers…

2

Pictures

How do you judge a picture? You could spend a lifetime studying art and still not understand a tenth of what there is to know. Every period has produced its artistic geniuses and while you may not have the Mona Lisa hanging above your mantelpiece you could be looking at something that has more than just sentimental value. So whether it's an oil painting, a watercolour, a pencil drawing or an etching, a little bit of basic knowledge and research will soon put you on the right track.

This chapter will show you how to distinguish an original painting from a print, how to go about researching the artist, and how to assess the condition of a picture and look after it.

What is it?

The first thing to do when assessing a picture is to establish whether it is an original painting or a print. Look at the picture close-up, using a magnifying glass if necessary, and focus on a small section. If you can see a series of very small, regular dots, uniformly spaced, you are looking at a print.

If it's an original, the next thing to check is the artist's signature. This can be anywhere on a picture but the traditional position is the bottom right-hand corner. A signed work of art is so much easier to research than an unsigned one but in either case you need to be aware that there are a lot of fakes and forgeries about. If you think you have discovered something of value, consult an expert.

Artists who sign their work will usually add the year in which they completed the piece. In the nineteenth century it was common to represent the date using the last two digits only, so the year 1887 would be shown as '87. During the twentieth century it was more usual give the year in full, e.g. 1987.

A series of letters after a signature will often indicate that the artist was or is a member of a particular society. There are dozens of these in Britain alone and the one that most people have heard of is the Royal Academy. So if you find the letters RA after the artist's signature you will have every reason to get excited because you will be able to trace the work's provenance. (See page 25 for a list of well-known societies of artists.)

Researching a picture

If you have a signed and dated original painting, and you are able to decipher the signature and so identify the artist (not always an easy thing to do), you should contact a reputable auction house and ask whether the artist is listed.

If so, their fine-art expert should be able to give you:

- basic biographical details about the artist – nationality, dates of birth and death, general style of his/her work, usual genre, e.g. watercolour landscapes, portraits in oils, etc., typical subject matter, etc.

- information about when and where the artist did most of his/her work
- details of when and where the artist exhibited
- a list of the artist's best-known works
- confirmation of whether anything by the artist has been sold at auction recently and how much it fetched

An auction house should not charge anything for giving you this basic information, although you should expect to pay a fee if you ask them to provide a written valuation for insurance purposes. Once you have established that you have a work of art by a listed artist, ask the auction house if they would like to see it. You can offer to take it in to them or if that is not convenient, a series of photographs will usually be acceptable in the first instance. Try to offer as much additional information about the work as you can, including: dimensions of the picture, its general condition, information about how, when and where you acquired it and its provenance.

There is nothing to stop you doing your own research, of course, using reference books and the internet. A word of warning about the internet, though: most of the material you are likely to come across will be unofficial and unregulated, so don't assume that everything you read is true or accurate.

Prints

Prints fall into one of three categories: standard prints, limited-edition prints and etchings.

Standard prints are mass-produced, so prepare yourself for a disappointment. They are often reproductions of famous paintings, run off and sold in their thousands. Unless your print falls into that special area of pop and rock or film memorabilia, you can be sure that ninety-nine times out of a hundred the frame will be worth more than the picture.

Limited-edition prints are exactly what they say they are: prints that have been reproduced mechanically but only a specified or guaranteed number of times. So somewhere on the print, usually at the bottom, towards the right-hand corner, you should find two sets of numbers separated by a forward slash, e.g. 75/1000. The second number indicates how many copies were made altogether and the first number tells you which particular copy you are currently looking at. So 75/1000 means that this is copy number 75 of a work that was issued in a limited edition of 1000 copies. If the artist has been honest, this offers you a guarantee that tells you how many copies of the work exist and this promises a certain rarity value. A further safeguard is for the artist to sign each copy individually by hand, and sometimes the printer will mark each print with an embossed stamp to give added authenticity. Photographs are often released onto the market in this way as well as prints taken from original paintings or drawings.

Etchings are prints produced by engraving an image onto a metal plate, often copper, which is treated with acid and then coated with ink. This technique was first developed in the early sixteenth century and has been popular with artists ever since as a way of reproducing their work. It is a monochrome process so if you find an etching with colour on it, it will have been touched up by hand after the print was made. The etched plate leaves an impression around the image, which is how you can distinguish an etching from an original pencil or pen and ink sketch. There is no limit to the number of prints that can be run off using this method.

Looking after a picture

While a picture is still in your possession, make sure you follow a few basic rules for looking after it, whether it is hanging on the wall or packed away in storage.

Do not expose your pictures to strong sunlight or direct heat. It may be tempting to hang a picture above a mantelpiece but if you have an open fire you are inviting damage from the heat and smoke. Heat from radiators and cigarette smoke can also be harmful.

When storing a picture or if you want to transport it, always wrap it on its own in a soft packaging material such as bubblewrap and then stack it vertically.

Restoration

My advice about do-it-yourself restoration is: don't. You could end up wiping off an awful lot of a picture's value along with the dirt. Restoration and cleaning is a highly specialized skill and is best left to the experts. The only thing you could safely do yourself is to replace the glass if it is broken. Leaving parts of a picture exposed to the atmosphere or light will cause harmful stains and fading. Don't worry if the picture frame is tatty or damaged, though, as a poor frame will not detract from a picture's overall value – indeed, if it is the original one then this will only enhance it, whatever condition it is in.

Assessing the condition of a picture

The general condition of a work of art will affect its value. When assessing a piece look out for signs of the following: tears and rips, re-canvassing and foxing.

Tears and rips are not always immediately obvious in an old painting, especially in the darker sections, so always check the back of the picture if possible as well as the front.

Re-canvassing is usually a bad sign. The canvas of an original old painting should betray its age, maybe cracked and faded in places, with traces of dirt and dust. If part of the canvas is clearly new, you should look for signs of restoration; if the whole canvas is new then you should be even more suspicious – your picture is probably a copy.

Foxing occurs when paper gets damp and the result is a lot of little disfiguring brown specks. It typically occurs on books, prints and watercolours.

Societies of artists

When an artist adds a series of letters after his/her signature it usually indicates that he/she is a member of a society. The initials of a selection of well-known societies of artists are listed below.

ARA   Associate of the Royal Academy

ARCA   Associate of the Royal Cambrian Academy

ARHA   Associate of the Royal Hibernian Academy

ARPE   Associate of the Royal Society of Painters and Etchers

ARSA   Associate of the Royal Scottish Academy

ARSW   Associate of the Royal Scottish Watercolour Society

ARWS   Associate of the Royal Watercolour Society

BWS   British Watercolour Society

FRS   Fellow of the Society of Antiquaries

LG   London Group

NA   National Academy of Design (New York)

NSA   New Society of Artists

OWS   Old Watercolour Society

PS   Pastel Society

RA   Royal Academician

RBA   Member of the Royal Society of British Artists, Suffolk Street (SS)

RBC   Royal British Colonial Society of Artists

RBSA   Member of the Royal Birmingham Society of Artists

RCA*   Member of the Royal Cambrian Academy, Manchester

RE   *See* RPE

RHA   Member of the Royal Hibernian Academy, Dublin

RI   Member of the Royal Institute of Painters in Watercolours (formerly NWS)

RIBA   Member of the Royal Institute of British Architects

RMS   Royal Society of Miniature Painters

ROI   Member of the Royal Institute of Painters in Oil-colours

RP   Royal Society of Portrait Painters

RPE   Member of the Royal Society of Painters and Etchers (later RE)

RSA   Member of the Royal Scottish Academy

RSW   Member of the Royal Scottish Watercolour Society

SS   *See* RBA

SWA   Society of Women Artists

WIAC   Women's International Art Club

* Not to be confused with the Royal College of Art, London, which has the same initials.

3

Furniture

All furniture tends to be expensive if it is made entirely from one type of solid wood but furniture-makers have always known how to keep the cost down. The usual way of making a piece look more expensive than it really is is to use veneers. In the old days this was a case of taking a native and therefore relatively cheap wood like oak and then veneering it with something more exotic and costly like mahogany or satinwood. In today's world of MDF, chipboard and flatpack self-assembly furniture, solid oak is a luxury but 250 years ago it was commonplace.

Furniture design really took off in Britain in the middle of the eighteenth century and part of the inspiration was these new woods coming in from the Caribbean, South America and India. It was the golden age of Chippendale, Sheraton and Hepplewhite, whose craftsmanship has never been bettered. This chapter will help you to identify the styles associated with these designers and those who came after them, including Charles Rennie Mackintosh, who created the chair pictured opposite.

Styles and periods

Styles in furniture over the years have reflected the changing fashions in architecture and design. Being able to recognize the period styles is key to identifying when a piece of furniture was made.

The Rococo style predominated during the eighteenth century and the furniture of this period reflects this, with elaborate scrolling, floral and shell inlaid decoration and curved legs. Gilding was also a favoured technique. Furniture-makers were still using native woods during the early part of the century, such as oak, ash, elm, walnut and yew, but as the British Empire developed they had more exotic woods to choose from.

Mahogany was first introduced from Jamaica in the 1730s. It was particularly admired for its unusual deep red colour and the fact that it could be polished to a very high shine. It was also very hard-wearing and was resistant to woodworm. Calamander, known as 'zebra wood', was shipped in from India's Coromandel coast, as was rosewood.

By the end of the eighteenth century the somewhat florid Rococo style had given way to Neoclassicism, with its straighter lines and less fussy decoration, and swags and bows were often a feature on pieces of this time. Imported mahogany was still popular but native walnut, oak, elm and beech were not neglected. Important furniture-makers of this period include Thomas Chippendale, Thomas Sheraton and George Hepplewhite.

Thomas Chippendale (1718–79), the son of a carpenter, came from Otley in West Yorkshire. He moved to London in 1738 and opened a furniture shop. Although he made all types of furniture he is best known for his chairs. In 1754 he published a book called *The Gentleman and Cabinet-Maker's Director*, cataloguing many of his designs. His furniture is so elegant that it is not surprising that he was often copied during his lifetime and is still influential today.

Thomas Sheraton (1750–1806) made elegant furniture in the Neoclassical style. His pieces are very slender, having thin, tapered legs giving the impression of delicacy although their construction is actually strong and sound (see page 16). He used mostly mahogany with satinwood for the inlaid shells, ovals, urns and straight lines known as 'stringing'.

George Hepplewhite (1721–86) was an English cabinetmaker who started his working life as an apprentice to the English furniture-maker Robert Gillow of Lancaster. Like Chippendale, Hepplewhite went to London and opened a shop there. However, his pieces are more like those of Thomas Sheraton, often incorporating inlaid shells, urns, etc. He is best known for his chairs with shield-shaped backs, and his trademark motifs are carved ears of wheat and Prince of Wales feathers. Two years after he died his wife published a book containing nearly 300 of his designs entitled *The Cabinet-Maker and Upholsterer's Guide*.

**A Hepplewhite chair with its distinctive
shield-shaped back**

Thomas Hope (1769–1831) was born in
Holland and came to Britain in 1795. He was
a collector of antiques and an interior designer.
His furniture designs were in the Regency
style and were intended for everyday use
and comfort. One of his innovations was
the sabre leg or Waterloo leg, based on
the curved shape of a cavalry sword.

Rococo was definitely passé by the
beginning of the nineteenth century, though
the Neoclassical style was still popular.
Eventually the characteristic delicate, slim-
legged pieces gave way to the much darker,
larger, sturdier-looking furniture that we
associate with the Victorian era.

By the time Queen Victoria came to the
throne in 1837 furniture-making had become
in part a mechanized process. Her reign
saw the rise of the bourgeoisie and the
development of greater comfort in their
homes. Rooms started to look cluttered, with
every available space taken up with furniture,
pictures and ornaments. This was good
news for the manufacturers, who supplied
the heavy, well-made tables and chairs,
sofas, sideboards, cabinets, desks, beds
and wardrobes.

Important furniture-makers of this period
include Thomas Hope, William Morris and
Charles Rennie Mackintosh.

William Morris (1834–96) was one of the
pioneers of the Arts and Crafts movement
and also one of the most commercially
minded. He designed furniture, textiles, wallpaper and books according to the movement's
aesthetic principles of the perfect match of
form and function. His Sussex chair, a 'rustic'
piece made of English ash, with carver arms
and a rush seat, is a classic example of the
style. His hand-printed wallpaper and fabrics,
with their colourful, swirly flowers and peacock
feather motifs, were reproduced in a popular
revival of his designs in the 1980s.

Charles Rennie Mackintosh (1869–1928)
was born in Scotland and was an architect
as well as a furniture-maker. Like William Morris,
he embraced the Arts and Crafts ethos and
he managed to make everything he designed
look totally distinctive. His designs, which
were heavily influenced by his architectural
background, combined straight and gently
curving lines to create pieces that were more
decorative than practical. There is no mistaking
his work – who would ever forget the shape
of a typical Mackintosh chair with its exag-
geratedly high back (shown on page 26)?

Pine

Pine furniture has been produced for several centuries but became widely used in the late nineteenth century as a cheaper alternative to oak. It was often used as the base wood to a veneered piece. Pieces made entirely from pine were usually painted to protect the wood from warping.

Only in relatively recent times has the wood been treated in a way that leaves the grain exposed. Although this fashion has made pine very collectable, in many cases the value of early pieces is similar to pieces being made today.

By the beginning of the twentieth century the industrial city of Nancy in northeastern France had established itself as the main centre for the production of furniture in the Art Nouveau style. The focus switched to Scandinavia during the 1920s and '30s when the sensuous fluidity of Art Nouveau gave way to the less sentimental 'jazz age' style of Art Deco. This was the period when some furniture-makers turned their backs on natural wood and started to experiment with new materials such as chrome, aluminium, steel and an early form of plastic known as Bakelite.

Utility furniture

During the Second World War many homes and their contents were damaged or destroyed by bombing and from 1943 the Treasury decided that all new furniture would be exempt from purchase tax (the forerunner of VAT) to make it more affordable. And so the British people were introduced to the concept of 'one size suits all, take it or leave it' furniture. Every piece that came out of Britain's factories had a 'Utility' mark stamped on it. During this time all manufacturing was under government control to make sure that every industry was contributing to the war effort. It was the first time in the country's history that the government had ever been responsible for the design and assembly of the nation's furniture.

The 'Utility' mark was rather in the style of two 'Pac-Man' figures. It had already been applied to clothing and consumers soon got used to seeing it on everything they bought, even wedding rings. The government controlled the use of gold and silver during the war and most wedding rings of the period carried an extra hallmark in the shape of an incomplete 'O', which was a guarantee of quality.

Utility furniture was built to strict specifications that made the most economical use of materials and labour, but even though it was extremely plain to look at, it was well designed and well made. It proved to be quite popular, being sold well into the 1950s, so there is now a lot of it about, especially as many people are now beginning to inherit it from their parents or grandparents, who set up home during the Second World War. There is a growing band of enthusiastic collectors so there is a market for it even if the prices are not exceptional.

Modern furniture

From the 1970s some designers took their inspiration from the space race and they produced items of furniture that suited the mood, using 'futuristic' materials.

Influential furniture-makers of the twentieth century include: Louis Majorelle, Gerald Summers, Marcel Breuer and Harry Bertioa.

Louis Majorelle (1859–1926) was one of the most prominent makers of Art Nouveau furniture in France. His work was exclusive, most of his pieces being made to order.

Gerald Summers (1899–1967) is famous for Art Deco furniture, in particular open armchairs made from laminated birchwood.

Marcel Breuer (1902–81) was one of the first designers to make furniture from materials other than wood. His most famous design is the 'wassily' chair, which has a tubular steel frame with leather straps for the seat, back and armrests. It is a design that has remained popular to the present day and can be loosely compared to the director's chair that we all recognize.

Harry Bertioa (1915–78) was an Italian sculptor who worked for the Knoll factory in America in the 1950s, designing functional sculptures. One of his most famous furniture designs is the 'diamond' chair. The frame is made from welded steel rods, criss-crossed into small diamond shapes. Some of these chairs came with a detachable vinyl seat. Bertioa described this chair as being made mostly from air, but able to levitate a person.

Makers

Only rarely do identifying marks provide proof of origin and very many designs were copied close to the time of the original or reproduced by later craftsmen to a standard equal to that of the original piece. Furniture is rarely 'signed' by a maker, so usually the layperson (and in many cases the dealer) will have to consult an expert to establish the maker and authenticity. Just occasionally, however, written evidence will supply the necessary provenance to a famous maker and in these cases the value will be greatly enhanced.

Valuation

Valuing a piece of antique furniture is best left to the experts as even slight differences in appearance, style or condition can affect the price of pieces that are otherwise the same. Does your desk still have all its original drawers and handles, for example, and is your Edwardian chaise longue still stuffed with horsehair? Are your six dining room chairs a true set or is one of them a clever copy, and do they really match the table? A lot of pieces are 'marriages' and a professional should be able to tell the difference.

Original or reproduction?

The first thing to do with furniture is to establish the style of the piece. However, this will not necessarily give you an accurate date as many of the classic designs of the past have been reproduced. The clue lies in the materials used and the techniques of construction as reproductions are nearly always of inferior quality.

There are many ways in which an expert is able to establish the age of a piece of furniture. But in most cases, reproductions have features that are glaringly obvious, for example, machine-made screws or the giveaway striped effect of modern plywood.

A handy tip for dating pieces with drawers is to look at the dovetailing. Drawers made in the early part of the eighteenth century are usually held together with two dovetail joints at each right angle while later pieces might have four, five or even seven.

4

Pottery and porcelain

Every civilized society has known about making pottery, even if only in crude form, and the fragments that archaeologists dig up can tell us a lot about everyday life in ancient times. But the production of fine china is a different matter altogether. By the time the great European porcelain factories such as Meissen, Sèvres and Chelsea had established themselves in the eighteenth century, China had known the secret for over 1600 years. The Ming dynasty (1368–1644), a period responsible for producing some of the finest porcelain ever seen, was already over.

However, once the potteries in the West had got their hands on this china from the Far East and had figured out how to make it themselves, there was no stopping them. Josiah Wedgwood, Josiah Spode, John Doulton, John Wall of Worcester and countless others started companies that are bywords for quality English china to this day.

Collecting pottery and porcelain can be great fun. There is so much to choose from, it can be useful as well as beautiful and not all of it is expensive. However, if you are thinking of selling, you should be aware that serious collectors are looking for perfection so a damaged piece will not usually be worth very much unless it is very old or very rare. If you hear of something being described as of 'decorative value only' then you will know it is chipped or cracked and worth very little.

Checking china

When you are considering whether to sell your china, the first thing to do is to determine whether it is pottery or porcelain. As a general rule, pottery looks rougher and feels heavier. Hold your piece up to the light – is it trans-lucent? If so, then it is probably porcelain. Porcelain will produce almost a ringing tone if you flick it with your fingernail while pottery will give off a dull, unmusical sound.

The next thing to do is to inspect the item carefully to see if it is damaged in any way. Look for any obvious signs of repair. Broken china can be mended with glue but after a while this can turn a yellowy-brown colour, drawing attention to the join. You may not notice any repairs if they have been done really well by a professional restorer but an expert can usually spot the signs. If the piece is made of porcelain hold it up to the light – this will usually reveal any serious cracks.

Run your hands systematically all over a piece to feel for any chips, especially around edges, where most accidental damage is likely to occur. Finally, place the piece on the palm of one hand and hold it there firmly. Give it a gentle tap with a fingernail of your other hand. What do you hear? With a porcelain piece, a clear, ringing sound will tell you that the piece is almost certainly fine, whereas a dull sound may be an indication of damage.

How to identify and date ceramics

Identifying and dating ceramics can be tricky. The first thing to check is whether there are any markings on the underside of the piece.

These could be: a maker's mark, a patent mark (a design registration mark or a kite mark), an individual decorator's mark, a retailer's mark, and pattern, model or shape numbers. After 1891 all pottery and porcelain, both home-produced and imported, had to be stamped with a country of origin. It was later decided that the words 'made in' should precede this to avoid possible confusion with pattern names.

Makers' marks

Most manufacturers stamp their china with their own individual maker's mark, and this is usually just the factory name, but some makers adopt a special monogram or symbol. It's always useful to be able to recognize these and the following is a selection of some of the more famous makers and their marks that you are likely to encounter.

A few factories chose to leave their china completely unmarked. In some cases this was because they were copying the designs of prominent manufacturers, making cheaper versions using poorer quality materials. On large dinner services it was common practice to mark only the largest or most important pieces. When sets are split these pieces can become separated from the rest, making identification of the remaining smaller items more difficult.

Patent marks

Patent marks were introduced in the UK in 1842 so that manufacturers could register and protect their designs and prevent their competitors from copying them. Once a factory had registered its design, the patent was valid for five years. The first patent mark was in the shape of a kite and this is how the term 'kite mark' was coined. Once you have learned how to decipher a kite mark on a piece of pottery you will be able to tell exactly when it was patented.

The diagram below shows the positions of the letters representing the class (quality), year, month and day in kite marks for designs patented between 1842 and 1867. The 'parcel' number, which is similar to a modern batch number, is also shown, but this is only really relevant to the manufacturer and has no bearing on the date or value.

The following table tells you which letter of the alphabet was allocated to which year for the period 1842 to 1867. As you will see, the choice was not sequential but random.

A = 1845	B = 1858	C = 1844
D = 1852	E = 1855	F = 1847
G = 1863	H = 1843	I = 1946
J = 1854	K = 1857	L = 1856
M = 1859	N = 1864	O = 1862
P = 1851	Q = 1866	R = 1861
S = 1849	T = 1867	U = 1848
V = 1850	W = 1865	X = 1842
Y = 1853	Z = 1860	

Naturally, the letters of the alphabet had been used up after the initial run of 26 years, so the potteries solved the problem by changing the position of the date marks. For the next 16 years the order was as follows, and again the letters selected were out of sequence:

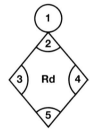

1868–83

Rd = Registered
1 = class (quality)
2 = day
3 = parcel number
4 = year
5 = month

A = 1871	C = 1870	D = 1878
E = 1881	F = 1873	H = 1869
I = 1872	J = 1880	K = 1883
L = 1882	P = 1877	S = 1875
U = 1874	V = 1876	X = 1868
Y = 1879		

Remember that these letters indicate the year when a design was patented and this is not necessarily the same as the year a piece was

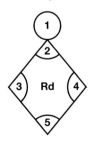

1842–67

Rd = Registered
1 = class (quality)
2 = year
3 = month
4 = day
5 = parcel number

made. It is also useful to note that ceramic items are never marked with an actual date of manufacture. If you do see a piece with a date marked on it, for example, 'Coalport Porcelain 1750 AD', then you should be aware that this indicates the year when the company was founded.

In 1884 the industry abandoned the kite mark in favour of a numerical system. Unfortunately, the numbers following the letters 'Rd' or 'Rd no' (registered number) referred to each new design rather than the year it was patented but the following chart will help:

1884–1910	
1884–1889	1 – 120,000
1890–1895	120,000 – 250,000
1896–1900	250,000 – 350,000
1900–1905	350,000 – 450,000
1905–1910	450,000 – 550,000

Decorators' marks

There are some artists who worked as designers for British potteries who have now become quite famous. They would often autograph their pieces, either by name or personal monogram, in the same way that a fine artist signs a painting. If a piece is attributed and signed this can greatly increase its value. There are several well-known British ceramic designers and decorators whose work is now highly prized and extremely collectable. These include: Charlotte Rhead, who worked for the Crown Ducal factory; Hannah Barlow, best known for her pastoral scenes featuring cattle for Doulton Lambeth (later Royal Doulton); John Stinton, who also specialized in cattle scenes, but for Royal Worcester; Keith Murray, who developed a trademark style for Wedgwood that was typically Art Deco, usually plain white; and Clarice Cliff, perhaps the most celebrated of all twentieth-century ceramic artists, who designed for Wilkinson's and Newport.

Whenever the reigning monarch visited a pottery or purchased items from them they conferred on those manufacturers the right to add the word 'Crown' or 'Royal' to their company name.

Kite mark quiz

Below is a selection of kite marks and registration numbers. See if you are able to date them. (The answers are on page 141.)

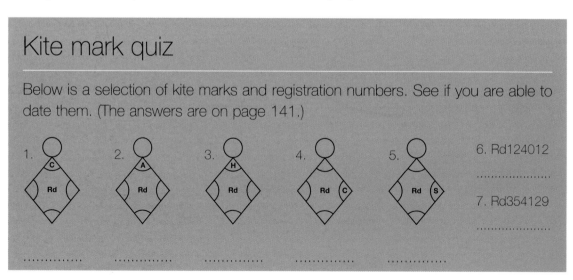

6. Rd124012

....

7. Rd354129

....

Additional marks

Pattern or model numbers often appear on a piece when there are no makers' marks or patent numbers. These are like stock numbers and they refer to a specific design and range of merchandise. Pattern numbers should not be mistaken for an actual date.

Shape numbers identify a particular piece, say a saucer, within a range of pieces making up a set such as a tea service. This allows retailers to specify exactly what they want when ordering items from the manufacturer.

Retailers' marks in the form of a company name or logo are an indication of a special trading relationship between a supplier and a buyer. Businesses and other organizations often had some form of corporate identity marked on their china if they bought in bulk. Depending on the particular connection, pieces marked in this way are often very collectable.

Looking after your china

Restoration

One of the earliest ways of restoring china, before the invention of suitable adhesives, was to put metal staples over the cracks to bind the piece together. This form of repair is very visible and appears quite crude but it can be effective and long-lasting. And at least there is no attempt to disguise the damage and it shows the piece in an honest state.

The cost of professional restoration can be very high and will do little to increase the value so I recommend it only for items that you treasure and want to keep.

Cleaning china

It is always worth keeping china clean and you don't need anything special – just warm soapy water and a soft cloth. Be especially careful with anything that has been hand-painted or you may rub the decoration off the piece and literally pour its value down the drain. Don't be tempted to use strong detergents, soap-filled pads or pan-scrubs – they are abrasive and can easily damage the surface of china. And steer clear of the dishwasher. Old china was not designed to cope with water being jet-blasted at it at very high temperatures. I find it is always best to wash china in a bowl on a table away from the sink. That way you won't accidentally bash a treasured cup or teapot on the kitchen taps. If you have trouble with really stubborn stains, for example in a jug or vase, try filling it with water, dropping a denture-sterilizing tablet in and leaving it overnight.

Packing and storing china

Wrap every item individually, even the lids – old newspaper is ideal for this – and stack plates vertically. China responds quite well to variations in temperature and humidity so it can be stored almost anywhere. I am no advocate of wire plate-hangers as the grips can dig in and leave marks on a piece but if you want to move or store a piece, leave the grips in place. They can be quite tricky to remove and you risk cracking a plate if you are not careful.

Top of the pots

From among the many thousands of potteries that have produced millions of pieces of pottery and porcelain over the years I have selected a handful that I feel are the most interesting and worth collecting. Here are my top ten, in reverse order: Staffordshire, Wade, Pendelfin, Charlotte Rhead, Spode, Clarice Cliff, Moorcroft, Royal Worcester, Beswick, Doulton. It is no surprise that so many of these manufacturers made their base in Staffordshire, as the county was the largest natural source of clay in Britain.

10. Staffordshire

One type of china from the Potteries that has always been popular is Staffordshire flatware. These pieces were flat at the back (hence the name) and were intended as shelf ornaments, so only the fronts had moulded features and decoration. The figures often come in mirror-image pairs, designed to stand on either end of a mantelpiece. Some of the early ones were adapted to serve as spill-holders.

Flatbacks are fired in simple moulds that produce a fairly crude basic shape, often with no fine detail on areas of a figure such as the hands. They have always been predominantly white but sometimes a little colour is added to features like the eyes. They are typically human figures or animals. Popular subjects in the nineteenth century were military heroes such as Lord Nelson and Napoleon; poets such as Robert Burns; characters from fairy tales, such as Little Red Riding Hood (with Wolf); and animals, both domestic and wild. Dogs have always been long-term favourites, especially spaniels, and they are still being produced today. Known sometimes as 'wally dogs', they usually come as matching pairs.

Desirable though they might be, old Staffordshire flatbacks are unlikely to be worth a fortune – prices range between £50 and £200. You might get more for a good pair of wally dogs and if you see a couple with added colour, gilded collar chains and separately moulded front feet, you could be looking at around £300. There are some pieces that collectors particularly look out for because they have inadvertently misspelled titles (pottery-makers and decorators were often illiterate), such as 'Cum Feed the Burds'. The rarest model of all, known as 'The Menagerie', is worth several thousand pounds. It was produced by Obadiah Sherratt (*d.* 1841), one of the few Staffordshire makers of this type of pottery known individually by name.

Flatbacks have never lost their popularity and they are still being made today. So how can you tell whether you have a modern reproduction worth £8–10 or a desirable antique that might fetch up to ten times as much?

Antique flatbacks have:

- a small air hole in the centre of the back
- quite dull-looking, subtle colours

- muted gilding
- random crazing in parts as a result of natural aging

Reproduction flatbacks have:
- quite a large air hole in the base
- bright colours
- very shiny intact gilding
- excessive, regular-looking crazing (the glaze is deliberately designed to craze all over to give the piece an 'antique' look)
- the painted eyes on spaniels sometimes appear slightly Oriental

9. Wade

George Wade started his pottery business in 1922 in Burslem. At first he produced tableware but the company's reputation rests on the range of figurines known as 'whimsies' that they introduced in 1954. When the Disney film *Lady and the Tramp* was released in 1956, Wade acquired the rights to reproduce china figures of the main characters. They issued six altogether: Tramp, Lady, Si, Am, Trusty and Jock. In the film, Lady arrives at the Darling household in a hatbox and so Wade took this idea and packaged the whimsies in miniature hatboxes. Today these figures are worth between £175 and £300 each – with the exception of Jock, who is valued at £500–800. Because Jock had a relatively minor role in the film, Wade did not make as many models of him as of the more popular characters. And rarity creates value. This is a general principle that you will find over and over in the antiques world and one that is well worth remembering if you are building up a collection in any sphere with a view to making a profit in the future.

Following their success with the Disney characters, Wade extended their range to include other cartoon film characters as well as straightforward figures of birds and other wildlife.

Most whimsies are quite small, just a few centimetres high. In the early days they were often put in Christmas crackers or included as free gifts on the front of comic books.

Between 1961 and 1965 Wade made slightly larger versions of their whimsies, known as 'blow-ups'. Approximately 10 cm (4 inches) high, these figurines are generally more valuable than the whimsies versions, with the most collectable being the *Lady and the Tramp* and the *Bambi* ranges.

In 1984 the National Westminster Bank offered a family of china piggy banks as free gifts to children under 12 as an incentive to get them to save. They commissioned Wade to make them and they have since proved to be quite collectable. The bank's young savers received a 'baby' pig when they first opened a savings account and they then went on to qualify for the rest of the piggy family (sister, brother, mother and father) if they reached a

Wade 'blow-up' of Jock the dog from Disney's *Lady and the Tramp*

series of pre-set targets within a certain period of time. As you would expect, many of them failed to save at the required rate and so there are more baby pigs in circulation than other members of the family. The babies are worth around £20–30 while the others emerge at between £30 and £80 apiece. A complete family of piggies in good condition would command a respectable £250 or so.

All the members of the piggy bank family had names. Can you remember them?
(The answers are on page 141.)

Baby: a) Woody b) Benny c) Toby
Sister: a) Susan b) Annabel c) Clara
Brother: a) James b) Maxwell c) Rupert
Mother: a) Lady Prudence b) Lady Cassandra c) Lady Hillary
Father: a) Sir Nathaniel b) Sir Cuthbert c) Sir Henry

8. Pendelfin

In 1953 two friends, Jeannie Todd and Jean Walmsley Heap, from Burnley, Lancashire, started making clay figurines and plaques in a garden shed. One of their main subjects was witches and they got their inspiration from nearby Pendle Hill, the location of a famous witch-hunt in the seventeenth century.

Todd and Walmsley-Heap chose the name Pendelfin for their company because they made elf figures as well as Pendle witches. However, they are now best known for the family of rabbits that they started to create in 1955. These cartoon-like characters wear clothes like people and are often depicted in human situations such as sleeping in a bed.

It has to be said that the early Pendelfin figures were not particularly well made. They tended to be top-heavy and would often fall over, so very few have survived undamaged. This is not a problem with the later figures and the rabbits, always their most popular line, are still in production today. The older pieces tend to be more valuable, especially the Father rabbit wearing a kipper tie from the 1960s (worth up to £300) and 'Shiner', from the same period, dressed in pink dungarees. The endearing thing about Shiner is that he is a rabbit with a black eye – he is currently worth around £400. The witch models and wall plaques did not originally sell as well as the rabbits but are now worth more.

7. Charlotte Rhead

Charlotte Rhead (1885–1947) was raised in the Potteries. Her father, Frederick Rhead, was a successful pottery decorator and he taught her the art of tube lining that William Moorcroft had perfected. She worked for various companies but is best known for the designs she created for Crown Ducal and Burgess and Leigh.

Charlotte Rhead joined Crown Ducal in 1931 and her work for them can be recognized by the stamp, which bears her name, the Crown Ducal logo and a pattern number. Her pieces are typically brightly coloured and often reveal a Persian influence in design. This is also reflected in the exotic names she chose for her ranges, such as 'Persino', 'Caliph' and 'Byzantine'. Her most common pattern is 'Golden Leaves' No: 4921 (not always signed, which makes it less desirable) and 'Persian Leaf' No: 5391. Depending on the rarity value of her pieces, a single plate can fetch anywhere between £150 and £600.

6. Spode

The Spode pottery was established by Josiah Spode in Stoke-on-Trent in 1770. His son and grandson, both also named Josiah, continued the factory until it was purchased by William Taylor Copeland and Thomas Garrett in 1833, which started what came to be known as the 'Copeland & Garrett' period. From 1847 it was known as 'Copelands Spode'.

The factory's original aim was to produce affordable decorative ceramics using a new process known as transfer printing. This is achieved by engraving a design onto a copper sheet that is then rubbed with ink. Paper is then placed over the copper so the image transfers onto it. The paper is then placed over the ceramic piece so the ink transfers. A glaze is then added to protect the design. This glazing was so effective that many eighteenth-century pieces have survived with their decoration in good condition to this day.

Once they had made a copper template china-makers found they could mass-produce things quickly, simply and cheaply – the key to any successful trade. Josiah Spode's head start over his competitors ensured his factory's position as Britain's largest manufacturer of transfer-printed pottery.

Willow pattern

Blue was one of the most common colours used in transfer printing because blue ink was made from cobalt oxide, which is very cheap and plentiful. And one of the best-loved designs of all time for blue on white

Spode willow pattern

china is the famous willow pattern. This clearly has a Chinese influence but it was actually created in Britain. It is commonly found on tableware and the value will depend on its age, condition, type of piece and maker.

The traditional willow pattern consists of a pagoda, a boat, a willow tree overhanging a three-arched bridge across which walk three Chinese figures, a fence in the foreground and two doves flying overhead. This scene is said to depict the story of Koon-See and Chang. Koon-See's father does not want her to marry Chang so the lovers run away, making their escape over the bridge and into a boat. They make it to another island and the father is about to catch up with them when the gods take pity and allow them to escape by turning them into a pair of doves.

Italian Spode

In the early part of the nineteenth century Spode merged with Copeland's, becoming Copeland's Spode. At this time the fashion for oriental patterns had largely given way to new European designs and Copeland's Spode developed a very successful range known as 'Copeland's Italian Spode'. This is now very collectable, especially the earlier pieces, which can be identified as the wording is enclosed in an oval, whereas on more recent items the words are unenclosed.

5. Clarice Cliff

Clarice Cliff (1899–1972) began work for the Wilkinson factory in Staffordshire in 1916, when she was just 16, where she trained as a modeller and decorator of ceramics. By 1930 she had set up her own studio in nearby Newport. Her work shows the influence of the popular Art Deco movement of the

Clarice Cliff's 'Red Roof' conical sugar sifter dates from the early 1930s and is now worth *c.* £4000

period, characterized by bold geometric shapes in bright primary colours. She designed mostly tableware for everyday use (though one would hesitate to bring a Clarice Cliff tea set out for breakfast these days) but also made a few ornamental figurines.

The patterns in her 'Bizarre' range, the most successful range of all, include 'Crocus', 'Blue Crocus', 'Orange Erin' and 'Inspiration'. All of her pieces are identified by a printed signature and are stamped either 'Wilkinson's' or 'Newport'. Some are also marked with the pattern name and a serial number.

Clarice Cliff is so fashionable these days that prices are very serious indeed. An 'Inspiration' sugar sifter could set you back more than £3000.

4. Moorcroft

William Moorcroft (1872–1946) worked for James McIntyre & Co in Staffordshire before setting up his own business in 1911. He

A typical Moorcroft vase from 1920, with brightly painted fruit over a blue ground glaze

3. Royal Worcester

Dr John Wall established his Worcester pottery in 1751 and he was allowed to change its name to Royal Worcester after a visit from King George III in 1789. At this time Chinese porcelain was being imported into Britain in large quantities. John Wall was impressed with the fine quality of these items from the Far East and felt that it was time to improve on the thick, heavy pottery that was pouring out of the Midlands at the time. After much trial and experimentation he became the first successful producer of British porcelain. The modellers at Royal Worcester based the shapes of their pieces on the British silverware of the day but they copied the Chinese colours and style of decoration.

For many years Royal Worcester were only able to produce items with blue under the glaze. These early pieces are now rare and you are more likely to come across the 'blush ivory' ranges. These were very popular in the nineteenth century. The porcelain was coloured to mimic ivory, a sort of yellowish beige with pink or blush highlights, and was usually gilded.

The reputation for quality that Royal Worcester have rests in part on the skilled modellers and decorators they employ. In the early days these artisans would be apprenticed from the age of 14 and schooled in anatomy and botany. They were encouraged to study the paintings of the old masters and some of them became masters themselves. Two famous Royal Worcester artists to look out for are John Stinton (1854–1956) and his second son, Harry (1883–1968). They specialized in scenes of Highland cattle, a typically romantic Victorian subject. John Stinton's first son, James

developed the art of decorating pottery called tube lining, which is a technique akin to icing a cake. This is where the outline of the design is 'piped' onto the ceramic piece using slip. The areas in between the lines are then filled with enamel paint and the whole design is fused when the piece is fired.

Moorcroft's pieces are distinctive as he tended to use very dark colours, usually with a floral theme. Pieces marked with 'William Moorcroft Potter to the Queen' date from between 1911 and 1935 – the monarch in question was Queen Mary. His most popular, and therefore least valuable, range is called 'Pansy', which was issued during the 1920s. If you happened to have anything from the 'Florian' range then you would be most fortunate, as this is considered to be the most desirable. But I think it is all so beautiful that everything is worth collecting, even the modern pieces that are produced in the Moorcroft factory today.

(1870–1961), was also an artist for Worcester and became well known for his portraits of game birds.

Another renowned Royal Worcester artist was George Owen, who specialized in a technique that involves piercing the porcelain. Unlike most artists who did this piercing using a mould as a guide, he made all the cuts by hand, relying entirely on his eye for measurement. Experts agree that Owen's artistry has never been bettered and his pieces are now worth many thousands of pounds.

Other artists associated with Royal Worcester whose work is highly collectable include: Charles Baldwin, Walter Sedgeley, Harry Davies, James Hadley and Eva Soper.

Dating Royal Worcester pieces

As with most companies, Royal Worcester use various marks and symbols to date their work. When the company was first founded in 1751, their blue and white china was either unmarked or marked with a crescent. From then until 1862, they adopted a variety of symbols and letters, the most common being a crescent moon. Following the introduction of this mark, a number of changes and alterations were made:

1891 The words 'Royal Worcester England' were added.

1892 A system of dots was introduced, with an extra dot being added each year until 1915, so, for example, a piece with seven dots puts the date at 1898.

1916 A star replaced the dots.

1917 The dots were reintroduced, along with the star, until 1927, so, for example, a piece with a star and four dots dates the piece to 1920.

1938 The words 'bone china' were added.

Royal Worcester have always produced very superior quality porcelain and current prices reflect this. Pieces made before 1938 are the most valuable but serious collectors also have a high regard for the work of Eva Soper, which was produced during the Second World War, a period normally associated with austerity and 'Utility' goods.

2. Beswick

Beswick has been based in Staffordshire since the late nineteenth century. The company are renowned for their animal figurines and their first real popular success was a model of the 1938 Derby winner, 'Bois Roussel'. Beswick's designer Arthur Gredington spent hours studying the horse, taking meticulous measurements of it from

A merino ram, designed by Arthur Gredington for Beswick in the 1960s and now worth around £700

every angle, and he made many drawings before the mould was made. The first Bois Roussel rolled out of the kiln in 1939 and is Beswick's all-time best-seller. It is still in production today and its popularity means that even the early ones will only fetch £40–50.

Attention to detail has always been Beswick's hallmark and their figures are all realistic replicas modelled on a real animal. They still specialize in horses, sometimes thoroughbreds with a rider, or as representatives of a breed, such as shire horses and Shetland ponies. Plain brown horses are generally worth less than those produced with distinctive colours and markings.

In the early 1950s Arthur Gredington started studying farm animals and he produced a range of bulls, cows, pigs, sheep and goats, some of which are now very collectable indeed. Their value all depends on how many were made and how many remain in circulation in good condition. As a general rule, the rarer the breed of animal, the more valuable the piece, so a Galloway bull from 1963–68 will fetch more (around £2000) than a dairy shorthorn from about the same period (around £800). If all you have is a Friesian cow then be prepared for as little as £50.

The same applies in the case of the dogs that Beswick have produced. These figures are aimed at breeders and owners and so the factory has always responded to demand by producing and selling more copies of the popular breeds. Of the 70 breeds that they have covered at one time or another, only the most common remain in production today. These include the bulldog, labrador, dachsund, old English sheepdog, spaniel, beagle and Jack Russell. The rare,

discontinued lines, not surprisingly, will command higher prices at auction.

Beswick have now reduced their cats to just two types – the Persian and the Siamese – and they have also given up on the wild animals. They have issued over 120 different species over the years, including zebras and a mythical unicorn, the latter produced during 1968 and 1969 and now worth around £600. And then there were the fish. If you find a Beswick fish in good condition, rejoice. Production ceased in 1975, and their fiddly fins and slender tails made them extremely vulnerable to accidental damage, so there won't be many good ones left.

Beswick stayed within the animal kingdom (more or less) when they acquired the rights to the lovable Beatrix Potter characters in 1947. It has proved an exceptionally lucrative range, so popular in fact that you can buy a Peter Rabbit that was made only a few months ago. Sadly, it will be worth no more tomorrow than you paid for it today. But hang on to it. If Peter ever goes out of production he could start appreciating in value.

Beswick have added a lot of new items to their range of fictional figures and they now do, among others, Alice in Wonderland, Snow White (plus all seven dwarves), Rupert Bear, Winnie the Pooh and the characters from The Wind in the Willows.

Altogether it amounts to a huge output but all the Beswick figures are stamped with a serial number and so with the right reference book by your side you should be able to identify and value them quite easily. The most valuable are those where the back-stamp is gold, indicating when they were first produced. Those with the brown back-stamp are less sought after.

1. Doulton

John Doulton (1793–1873) and his partner John Watts established a pottery and porcelain business in Vauxhall, south London in 1815, moving to larger premises in Lambeth in about 1850. Doulton's second son, Henry (1820–97), was apprenticed to the business from the age of 15.

During Henry's early years at the factory the long overdue call for improved health and sanitation had created a market for clay sewage pipes and porcelain sanitary ware and that was what Doulton's were producing. The company prospered but when Henry took over from his father in 1854 he decided to move into artistic ceramics. He started by employing students and graduates of the nearby Lambeth School of Art. He allowed these artists virtually complete freedom to express themselves as they wished and he selected them entirely on merit, neither gender nor physical disability being a bar to recruitment. Their work did not sell well initially and the company lost money. But instead of abandoning the project, Henry expanded it, converting some nearby cottages into studios where the modellers and artists would work alone, free of supervision. Top-class artists such as Hannah Barlow (BHB), George Tinworth (GT), who was illiterate but went on to achieve membership of the Royal Academy, and Frank Butler (FAB), who was deaf and dumb, were allowed to add their personal signatures. 'Doulton Art Wares' did start to sell eventually and they now fetch massive sums at auction.

Henry Doulton's innovations in ceramic art earned him a knighthood in 1887 and in 1901 Edward VII honoured the company with a warrant, which brought with it the right to add the 'Royal' to their name. By then they had won many international honours for their extended range of products that now included the attractive Sung and Chang wares, *rouge flambé*, character jugs and figurines. The most popular type of pottery that they produced was stoneware, which was rather thick and rough-cast, usually painted in dark and muted colours. The pieces are stamped underneath 'Doulton Lambeth' and the most desirable bear the initials of the designer. Production continued at Lambeth until 1956.

Figurines

Royal Doulton figurines are now the company's most successful products. The first ones they made were not particularly popular until Queen Mary visited the pottery in 1912. Rumour has it that she saw a figurine of a small child called 'Bedtime' and exclaimed, 'What a darling!' Recognizing that they had a source of publicity that no amount of money could possibly buy, Royal Doulton instantly remarketed the figure with its new name – 'Darling'. They sold thousands and the same model is still being made today. One of these figures from the 1920s would now be worth as much as £300. Look for HN1 on the bottom – these are the initials of Harry Nixon, who was originally in charge of painting the figures.

Other collectable figurines include the 'Balloon Seller', made from 1921 and still in production, and the 'Bunnykins' family of rabbits. But beware – these figurines are sometimes made in subtly different versions and this can alter their value quite significantly. For instance, there are several versions of 'Santa Bunnykins' in circulation but only one has a hole in his hat (made so that he could

'The Maori', an extremely rare Royal Doulton character jug from 1939, now worth around £8000

be hung on the Christmas tree). This particular model is now worth about fifteen times more than those without the hole!

Series ware

One of Royal Doulton's best artists and modellers, Charles Noke, came up with the idea of decorating everyday items such as cups, jugs, plates and teapots with a theme. They were quite cheap to produce, being transfer-printed. The first year, 1889, he chose the Isthmian Games and he selected a new theme every year until the outbreak of the Second World War. The company re-introduced the idea in the 1970s. The most popular themes now are the scenes from Dickens and the rarest are those showing motor cars, hot-air balloons and aircraft.

Character jugs

Unlike Toby jugs, which are whole body caricatures, a character jug is a model of just the head and shoulders. The handle on the side is usually incorporated into the overall design. In 1930 the innovative Charles Noke designed Doulton's first character figure and he chose John Barleycorn, the embodiment of strong malt liquor in popular folklore, and cast him as a jolly fat man with a round red face. His John Barleycorn jugs are now worth about £70 – look for serial number D 5327.

Other figures quickly followed. Winston Churchill was apparently so offended by the character jug modelled on him (not a very good likeness in his opinion) that Royal Doulton withdrew him from sale after about 18 months and so they are very rare. Made in 1940 and 1941 with the model number D6170, they are worth between £5000 and £16,500. But if you find one with the model number D6849 it will only be worth about £50 because the factory started making them again in 1989 when Churchill was no longer around to complain.

'Old King Cole' (D6036) and the 'Granny' (D5521) are two designs to keep an eye out for; both were made in two versions. One of the Old King Coles, worth about £100, has a brown crown and these were made between 1939 and 1960; the other has a yellow crown, which, having been produced for just a few months at the beginning of the war (1939–40), is much rarer and therefore worth ten times as much. The same goes for the Granny jug: if she has a tooth she is worth about £45 but toothless could fetch nearly £500.

Royal Doulton character jugs and figurines are easy to identify. Every piece is stamped 'Royal Doulton (Made in England)', followed by the name of the character, the letters HN and the model number. Items produced before 1939 will also have the word 'potted' on the base.

5

Glassware

Glass sometimes occurs naturally, formed after volcanic eruptions, when rocks have been heated and then cooled rapidly. It is believed that man-made glass goes back to Egypt in the fourth century BC and there is evidence that the Syrians had invented an early glass-blowing technique by about 27BC. However, it was the Romans who discovered how to make glass transparent (in about AD100) by combining sand and potash (burnt wood). Roman glass has a green tinge and many imperfections and fragments still turn up from time to time. The first golden age of glass-making in Europe was in the thirteenth and fourteenth centuries when it became a true art in Venice; Venetian glass has had a high reputation ever since. The second occurred in England in the seventeenth century when George Ravenscroft added lead to the traditional mixture and created a pure, clear form of glass. He patented his idea under the name of 'lead crystal'. It proved a popular technique and in 1745 the government saw an easy way to raise some revenue and began to tax glassware, based on weight.

During the eighteenth century the levy had become so onerous that glass-makers looked for a way to produce lighter pieces. One clever tax avoidance trick was to make parts of an item hollow, for example the stem of a wine glass, so that it did not weigh so much. This period also saw a lot of coloured glass flooding onto the market as only clear glass was taxed.

Identifying glassware

The first step when identifying, dating and valuing glassware is to establish whether it is utility or art glass.

Utility glass is intended for everyday use and includes items such as bottles, wine glasses, decanters, jugs, bowls and even chandeliers. You could say that all glass was utility glass to begin with and it was not until the latter part of the nineteenth century that glass-makers began to produce so-called 'art glass', creating pieces that were purely ornamental or decorative, including jewellery.

Unlike pottery, glassware is not usually signed, stamped or dated, so you need to look for certain characteristic features to get some idea of its age. First of all, check whether the piece has a pontil mark. This is the uneven, slightly sharp lump that is left on the base where the glass-blower has snapped it off the rod. Hand-blown glass is likely to have bubbles or other imperfections in it and if a piece has scratches on the base they will appear slightly grey in colour. Machine-made glass is very uniform and all the items in a set will look perfectly matched.

Glass-making techniques

From the seventeenth century onwards glass production was a large and important industry all over Europe and manufacturers experimented with different styles, shapes, colours and designs.

The most common glass-making techniques are: cut glass, etched glass, moulded glass, coloured glass, flashed glass and cameo glass.

over the surface. It will feel noticeably sharp. The bad news is that even quite attractive old cut-glass items will probably sell for less than the cost of a brand-new equivalent.

Cut glass
One of the most popular methods of producing glassware with a decorative element. Cuts are made in the glass by a rotating metal wheel and the purpose and effect is to give it a brilliant finish that reflects light. You can identify cut glass simply by running a finger

Etched glass
Created by dipping the glass into an acid-resistant substance such as wax. A design is hand-carved into the wax and then the whole piece is submerged into hydrochloric acid, which eats away the exposed glass surface to give a characteristic white 'frosted' effect.

Moulded glass

The least valuable type of glass but it is probably the most practical for everyday items. It is easily identified by its smoothness to the touch and there is often a seam down the side of the piece. Being machine-made and mass-produced, plain moulded glass has little value.

Coloured glass

This has always been popular. The ancient Romans used it in their mosaics and the Christian church has been creating wonderful stained-glass windows for centuries. Colour is produced by adding metal oxides that cause a chemical reaction in the glass. Green glass is traditionally used for wine bottles and brown glass has always been favoured for beer but the most popular colours for decorative glassware are red, yellow and blue.

Red glass There are two main types of red glass – 'ruby' and 'cranberry' – both of which are very popular and highly collectable. As the name implies, ruby glass is dark red, the colour of rubies, and was originally created to be used as an imitation gemstone. In the early days most cranberry glass was produced in the USA and it was the American glass-makers who gave it the name because the pale pink colour reminded them of the juice of their native cranberries. One of the most sought-after types of cranberry glass is known as 'Mary Gregory'. No one knows who she was exactly but it is believed she was an employee of the Boston & Sandwich Co from Sandwich, Massachusetts, who

made cranberry glass. These pieces are quite distinctive as they are usually painted with white enamel and decorated with scenes involving children.

Yellow glass was first created around 1830, when scientists were experimenting with radioactive materials and discovered that uranium mixed with glass produced a yellow hue. Pieces that have survived today will still register on a Geiger counter (but not dangerously so) and are very collectable for their novelty value.

Blue glass is the most common colour for glass, probably because it is the cheapest to produce. The mineral that provides the colour is cobalt, which is widespread and easy to extract. Look out for glassware known as 'Bristol blue' – wine bottles and decanters made exclusively in the Bristol area during the eighteenth century. These pieces are very beautiful and extremely collectable.

Flashed glass

Produced by dipping plain glass into molten coloured glass. The glass-maker then creates a design by cutting through the coloured top layer to reveal the plain glass beneath.

Cameo glass

Produced in the same way as flashed glass, although usually with more layers of coloured glass, so that when it is etched by hand it produces very realistic pictures or designs. This glassware is highly collectable and consequently very valuable.

Utility glass

The earliest type of utility glassware you are likely to encounter in any quantity was produced in the eighteenth century and the various types of drinking vessel dating from this period are currently the most collectable.

These will be: ale glasses, wine glasses, cordial or liqueur glasses, coachman's glasses, custard cups and champagne bowls or flutes.

Ale glasses were mass-produced during the eighteenth century so they are among the most common and therefore least desirable pieces of this era. They look nothing like a modern beer glass or tankard but are similar in shape to a wine glass, though with a shorter stem and a larger bowl. Given the appalling lack of adequate sewage disposal during this period, it was probably safer to drink the ale than the water and a lot of taverns and private households brewed their own. The terms 'ale' and 'beer' are now used interchangeably but traditionally ale is brewed without hops.

Wine glasses were also mass-produced in the eighteenth century and were often decorated. There are dozens of different designs and shapes. To achieve a decent price they need to be in perfect condition, preferably in a matching set of at least six.

Coachman's glasses are quite distinctive as they consist of a bowl and a stem but no foot or base. They were used, it is said, to discourage travelling coach drivers from lingering too long in the tavern. Coachman's glasses would not stand up on their own and

so if you served someone a beer in one they could not put it down anywhere but had to keep it in their hand, which made them drink up quickly and leave straight away.

Custard cups, as the name suggests, were used for serving custard, which was a popular dessert in the eighteenth century. These glasses consist of a bowl with a looped handle set on a base. They would have been sold originally in sets of six and serious collectors are not interested in individual pieces on their own.

An eighteenth-century wine glass

Cordial or liqueur glasses are easy to spot as they have a very small bowl supported on a long stem. They usually only turn up in singles but are still quite collectable. Cordials and liqueurs are both spirit-based drinks flavoured with fruit and herbs and in the eighteenth century they were a favourite with the ladies, who drank in small quantities, hence the particular size shape of the glasses.

Champagne bowls or flutes are two very different styles of glass that have both been popular, depending on the fashion of the time. A champagne bowl has a base and a stem supporting a very wide, shallow bowl, while a champagne flute has a base and a tall, thin, slightly triangular bowl. Legend has it that Louis XVI designed the champagne bowl, getting his inspiration from the shape of Marie-Antoinette's breasts! Modern champagne-drinkers seem to prefer the flute shape,

An eighteenth-century cordial glass

as it is designed to keep the fizz going by stopping the bubbles from escaping too quickly. As with most types of drinking glass, champagne glasses are more attractive to the collector if they are offered in sets.

As well as drinking glasses of all kinds, utility glassware also comes in the shape of decanters, claret jugs, scent bottles, paperweights and chandeliers, all of which are well worth collecting if they are in good condition.

Decanters, claret jugs and tantaluses
Glass-makers have always made decanters and they are not just functional objects – many of them are very beautiful, which is why they are often put out on display in the home. Basically, a decanter is a glass bottle with a stopper; its purpose is to allow wine to be slowly transferred and then stored, without any sediment from an original container, such as a bottle or a cask.

As with all glassware, the first thing to do with a decanter is to check it for damage. The next thing to establish is whether you have the original stopper. This is not always easy and mismatches are common. A stopper should at least fit well into the neck of the decanter and if it does not then it will certainly be an imposter. Some decanters have a maker's mark, so if you find a serial number etched into the rim, you are in luck, because the original stopper will have the same number. Single decanters in perfect condition are collectable but are much more desirable if they come in pairs or sets of four or more.

One type of decanter to look out for is a ship's decanter, which is also called a Rodney decanter. The story goes that Admiral Rodney (1718–92) had his tunic ruined when red wine was spilt on it when a decanter fell over during a rough sea voyage. So he designed one with a large flat base that made it less likely to topple when the ship rolled. A Rodney decanter is highly collectable even as a single item.

In some households decanters were often locked away in wooden or metal-framed tantaluses. These were designed to display the contents while preventing the servants from getting drunk at their master's expense. The word 'tantalus' comes from a Greek myth, one version of which has the gods punishing Tantalus by submerging him in salt water up to his neck so that all he could see was water that he was unable to drink and so was 'tantalized'.

Decanters are not the only containers to be used for wine. Claret jugs are large jugs that sometimes have silver or pewter hinged lids. The glass is often highly decorated, which adds to the value. Claret jugs are very saleable and can be sold singly.

Scent bottles During the eighteenth and nineteenth centuries perfume was sold in very plain bottles, so people would immediately decant it into a decorative scent bottle that was attractive enough to sit on a dressing table. Scent bottles come in hundreds if not thousands of different designs and are not always easy to date. They are often made of cut glass with a band of silver around the neck. All British silver has a hallmark (see page 60) so this is one way of finding out how old a bottle is.

If you see a scent bottle made of coloured glass then try to find out what it is – as we have seen, cranberry glass or Bristol blue is very desirable. Look out, too, for double-

A Baccarat millefiori paperweight of c.1850

ended scent bottles, which are also very collectable. They have a compartment at one end for perfume and a vinaigrette at the other for smelling salts. A vinaigrette is a small gilt-lined metal box designed to hold a sponge soaked in spiced vinegar that would help to revive a lady who had fainted.

As you would expect, the condition of an antique scent bottle is all-important. Many bottles have ended up cracked and chipped as they were everyday objects in regular use. The stoppers are particularly prone to damage so you need to check, as with decanters, that they match the bottle. If you find that the stopper is stuck in the neck of the bottle, never try to force it out as you will almost certainly snap it off.

Paperweights, like scent bottles, are functional objects that can also be decorative and very beautiful. They were first made in the late nineteenth century and the most popular type is known as millefiori (from the Italian, meaning 'a thousand flowers'). This is a technique where several thin rods of coloured glass are bound together and then sliced very thinly. The slices are then covered over with clear glass in a solid dome. The resulting design is thus magnified and appears three-dimensional.

Three of the most famous manufacturers of paperweights are: Baccarat, identified by the letter 'B' or a horse's head; St Louis, marked 'StL'; and Clichy, which used a 'C' or a pink and green rose. Look for these initials and symbols on one of the 'petals' of the paperweight motif – an authentic piece by any of these makers is very collectable.

Chandeliers are large ceiling-mounted light fittings. They were often custom-made and so only very wealthy households could afford them. A chandelier is made up of three or more branches, each one holding a candle, and hung with multi-faceted decorative glass drops, known as lustres, which reflect the candlelight and so create extra illumination. There would also be a drip pan underneath to catch the hot wax when the candles were burning.

When first gas and then electric light was developed for domestic use, chandeliers were adapted to allow a gas pipe or electric cable to run through the branches and candles were abandoned.

Original candle chandeliers are rare and valuable. More recent versions are considered less attractive but there is still a market for them, though the average house would not have rooms large enough to take them.

Art glass

In contrast to utility glass, where form follows function, art glass is just the opposite: the form, design and decoration come first and any function is purely incidental.

So whether you're looking at a vase, a lamp or an ornament, the art glass designer intends your first response to be an aesthetic one – is it beautiful?

Names that you almost certainly already know – Louis Comfort Tiffany, René Lalique and Emile Gallé – are synonymous with fine art glass. These men were all pioneers, experimenting with revolutionary glass-making techniques such as *cire perdue* (meaning, literally 'lost wax') and favrile glass.

Louis Comfort Tiffany (1848–1933) was born into the jewellery trade – his father, Charles Louis Tiffany, established Tiffany & Co in New York in 1837 and his store for the rich and famous is still trading there today. Louis Tiffany is best known for his unique favrile glass and Art Nouveau designs. He was fascinated by the examples of Roman glass that he had seen and tried to re-create the same iridescent 'peacock feather' finish in his own pieces. His work is marked 'LCT' and most of it is now well beyond the pocket of the ordinary collector. His lamps are particularly popular and are worth thousands of pounds. (An example of one of his lamps, the 'Wistaria' design, is shown on page 16.)

René Lalique (1860–1945) was a French designer who specialized in jewellery, though he also produced other items, such as clocks and lamps and some furniture. His pieces were widely admired in his lifetime and they certainly fetch extremely high prices today. Like most designers working in the late nineteenth century, Lalique embraced Art Nouveau and he created brooches and combs in this style for the International Exhibition in Paris in 1900. His interest in glass design and manufacture began after he was approached by the French perfumers Coty, who asked him to design their scent bottles. He took enthusiastically to the new Art Deco style and some of his best-known work is from this period. His 'trademark' pieces are the blue-tinged opalescent vases that he designed in the 1920s using the *cire perdue* technique. His works have a moulded signature, 'R LALIQUE', underneath (which sometimes appears with the word 'France' and a model number), making them difficult to fake.

Emile Gallé (1846–1904) was best known for his complex cameo glassware. His designs, particularly those with a botanical theme, were influenced by the Art Nouveau movement. His signature (just the surname, Gallé) is found on the main body of a piece and is created using the same cameo glass technique.

These Lalique vases date from the 1920s and are now worth around £3000 each

Pale imitations

Most of us will never be able to afford anything by Tiffany, Lalique or Gallé, and let's face it, we are unlikely to stumble across their masterpieces in our attics, but these designers were very influential and we should not forget how good some of their followers were. In my opinion there are three producers who deserve a closer look: Sabino, the Northwood Glass Company and Daum Nancy.

Marius Ernest Sabino (1878–1961) was a French glass manufacturer based in Paris. His opalescent pieces are a homage to Lalique. Though clearly of poorer quality than the master, and unsigned, Sabino is nevertheless worth a second glance and can command quite respectable prices today.

The Northwood Glass Company was an American manufacturer that became famous for a type of glassware known as carnival glass. They developed a method of spraying glass with metal oxides to give a similar iridescent finish to the favrile glass that Tiffany had produced. But the main difference was that Northwoods shaped their glass ornaments in crude moulds and mass-produced them in their millions. Carnival glass was so cheap in the 1920s that the travelling funfairs (or carnivals as they were known in America) bought it to give away as prizes. Imitation Tiffany was everywhere and before long it was beginning to have an adverse effect on sales of the real thing.

Carnival glass made by the Northwood Glass Co is stamped with the letter 'N'. The most common, and therefore least valuable, pieces are the orange ones – a colour known as 'golden marigold' – and the green ones. The darker colours, like purple, are considered to be more attractive. Northwoods soon suffered from the imitators themselves as other glassworks realized there were huge profits to be made from carnival glass.

Daum is the name of a glass manufacturer based in Nancy in northeastern France. They imitated the work of Emile Gallé, who was also based in Nancy. The word 'Daum' can be found on the front of their pieces.

Novelty glass

Makers have been producing glass ornaments aimed at the tourist trade for years but that is not necessarily a bad thing – if you find a holiday souvenir in good condition from the nineteenth or early twentieth centuries then the price could be quite respectable. Novelty glass includes: Murano glass, Vaseline glass, end-of-day glass, agate glass and slag glass.

Murano glass comes from Murano, an island in the Venice Lagoon. It is very distinctive, being brightly coloured with lots of gold-leafing. A Murano clown figure from the 1950s could fetch up to £80 and a fish from the same period might come in at a useful £20.

Vaseline glass is an opaque glass that is trying to look like fifteenth-century Venetian glass. It gets its name from the fact this it looks as though it has had Vaseline rubbed all over it, giving it a slightly greasy-looking surface. It does not appeal to everyone but you might get £75 or so for a Victorian bowl.

End-of-day glass items are multi-coloured and the colours look as though they have been put together in no particular order. It is believed that at the end of the working day any left-over scraps of glass were melted down and used to make these pieces. If anything is a novelty then end-of-day glass certainly is and for a vase from the fashion-able 1930s you could be looking at a reasonable £50 or so.

Agate glass is multi-coloured and designed to look like carved agate. It fetches similar prices to end-of-day glass.

Slag glass is black and it gets its colour from the slag or coal dust that has been added to it. For those who like their old glassware in dark colours, prices are still quite modest. Expect around £100 for a vase from the 1880s.

6

Metalware

Metalware is the general term used to refer to anything made of metal or alloys. The main metals used for decorative objects are: silver and silver plate, Britannia metal, bronze and spelter, brass, copper, pewter and chrome. Being a precious metal, silver is generally regarded as the most desirable medium for most metalware. Silver is mined from the earth as ore and in its original state it often contains other metals, such as gold or copper. Pure silver is extremely soft so silversmiths will often mix it with enough copper to make it durable while retaining the pliability required to fashion it into intricate designs.

Silver and silver plate

It is important to know how to distinguish between solid silver and silver plate. Most experts can tell the difference just by handling an item but that is a skill that takes time and practice to acquire. While silver plate is still real silver, it is only a veneer, a thin layer fused over the surface of a base metal and so it is nowhere near as expensive or valuable as solid silver.

Fortunately, there are one or two simple ways of telling the two apart. First of all, look for any signs of wear. All silver needs regular cleaning to keep it shiny and in the case of silver-plated items this can lead to the thin surface layer being worn away, revealing the base metal underneath. You can easily test for this by breathing on the object. The condensation you have created will quickly show up any wear. If a metal of a different colour is showing through then you have silver plate. If it looks reddish in colour then you probably have Sheffield plate, as this is made with a copper base. This kind of show-through is known as bleeding.

The next step, if you are still not sure, is to look for any letters or marks impressed into the body of the object. The marks on objects made of silver or silver plate can be positioned anywhere (unlike ceramics, which are usually marked on the underside of the piece). On solid silver pieces you should look for the following: a British standard hallmark, a duty mark, a maker's mark and a kite mark or registration number. Silver plate does not have the same sort of hallmarks but should still have a stamp of some sort. Look out for the letters EPNS, EPBM or the name Sheffield. You will also need to know how to tell when a piece of silver is not British-made.

British standard hallmark

In the UK all silver items have to be checked to ensure they come up to a certain standard before they can be sold. By law British silver has to comply with what is known as a 'sterling silver standard', where the mixture has to be 925 parts silver to 75 parts copper or, in other words, 92.5% pure. This purity check takes place at the various assay offices in the country, the main ones being in London, Birmingham, Sheffield and Edinburgh.

When the assay office has verified the purity of a silver item, it allocates an assay mark (also known as a hallmark) to the piece, confirming that it is sterling silver. The hallmark also identifies the year of manufacture and indicates where the item was assayed.

The symbol that indicates that a piece is made from sterling silver is called a standard mark. There are three such marks for British silver: English silver is represented by a lion passant, Scottish silver by a thistle or a lion rampant and Irish silver by a crowned harp. (The whole of Ireland was part of the United Kingdom until 1922.)

Each assay office has its own unique symbol, too: the London office is represented by a leopard's head, and Birmingham, Sheffield and Edinburgh have, respectively, an anchor a crown and a castle. Legend has it that

English standard mark   **London assay mark**   **Birmingham assay mark**   **Sheffield assay mark**   **Edinburgh assay mark**

the original assayers from Sheffield and Birmingham met in a pub called the Crown & Anchor and looked no further for their logos.

The system of letters of the alphabet that the various assay offices have used over the centuries to indicate the date of a piece has become very complicated, especially as the practice of stamping hallmarks onto silver goes back as far as 1500. The chances of your finding a piece of sixteenth-century silver in your attic are probably pretty remote, so I shall concentrate on explaining my method of identifying some of the most common British date marks from around 1900 onwards.

The Birmingham assay office is well known for handling a lot of small silverware and so you are likely to come across its hallmarks quite a lot. First of all, look for its distinctive symbol, the anchor, then check for the lion that will indicate that the piece is English silver. When it comes to the date letter, we are lucky that Birmingham started off a new century with the first letter of the alphabet. So in the year 1900 they were using a lower-case 'a' within a square punch, shaped underneath. They then worked their way systematically through the alphabet (missing out the letter 'j' along the way), so the letter 'b' indicates 1901, 'c' is 1902, and so on.

In Sheffield the date letter for 1900 is a lower-case Gothic 'h' in a plain square punch. My trick for remembering this is to say that 'h' is for 'head', which reminds me of the crown that is Sheffield's individual assay office mark. Taking the letter 'h' to identify the year 1900, you can then work backwards to 1893, which is when the letter 'a' was first used, or forwards to 'i' for 1901. Like Birmingham, they missed out the letter 'j', so 1902 was shown with a 'k', 1903 with an 'l' and so on.

The mark of the Edinburgh assay office is a castle and the date letter for 1900 is a lower-case Gothic 't' (think 'turret') in an oval punch. They missed out the letters 'j' and 'u', so the year 1882 begins the cycle with 'a' and 1901 is 'v'.

For some reason the London assay office had to be awkward. Not only did it omit the 'j' like all the other offices, it also dropped the final five letters of the alphabet and only went as far as 'u'. Its date letter for 1900 is a lower-case 'e' in a square punch with a wavy bottom – I remember this as 'e' for *EastEnders* – and then the sequence operates in the same way as the others.

Other hallmarks you may come across include: Chester, Exeter, Glasgow and Newcastle.

British silver hallmark quiz

Below is a selection of assay and date marks from the period 1896–1915. See if you are able to identify the years they represent. (The answers are on page 141.)

1. ....   2. ....   3. ....   4. ....

5. ....   6. ....   7. ....   8. ....

Duty marks

Between 1784 and 1890 the British government imposed a duty on silver. This tax was collected by the Commissioner of Stamps, a body that later turned into the Inland Revenue. This gives collectors a useful clue when dating a piece from this period because it will be stamped with a duty mark in the form of a monarch's head to indicate that the tax has been paid. So you may come across the profile of George III, William IV or Queen Victoria. Victoria reigned for such a long time that her duty marks appear in two versions. The only time you are likely to find a duty mark on twentieth-century silver is on pieces made specifically to commemorate a significant royal event, such as a coronation or jubilee.

Makers' marks

Sometimes, before the hallmark, you will find letters representing the manufacturer. These can sometimes add value to a piece if the manufacturer was prominent. I have listed below some of the important makers whose work is very collectable:

Hester Bateman (1704–94) is regarded as one of the finest silversmiths of the late eighteenth century. She specialized in flatware (cutlery). Her sons carried on her trade and any silverware made by the Bateman family is very collectable today.

Elkington and Co (est. *c.*1830) were the pioneers of electroplating and are best known for their decorative and flamboyant pieces.

Archibald Knox (1864–1933) was a designer who worked for Liberty & Co. His designs are typical of the Arts and Crafts period and he drew inspiration from the Celtic decorative tradition. His most famous range is known as 'Cymric'.

Charles Asprey worked during the late nineteenth and early twentieth centuries. He was regarded as one of London's leading silversmiths and was a direct descendant of the founder of the famous London jewellery firm founded in 1781.

Kite marks and registration numbers

Prominent manufacturers often registered their designs with the patent office in order to establish copyright and to stop others from pinching their ideas. The patent office would issue a unique kite mark or registration number that would be stamped on every item. This system is the same as the one that was adopted by the potteries for their china (see page 35).

Foreign silver marks

If you find a three-digit number stamped on a piece of silver, this tells you that the piece has been imported into Britain. This number, known as a purity mark, represents the ratio of silver to other metals. The most common is 925 (which comes up to the British standard) but can be as low as 600.

If you are thinking of selling an item of imported silver, be warned that it may go for a considerably lower price than an equivalent British piece. This is because British silver is acknowledged as amongst the finest (and therefore most collectable) in the world.

Britannia silver

Britannia silver is a higher-grade silver (950) introduced in the late seventeenth century to combat clipping. This practice involved the illegal removal of small clips of silver from coins. The clippings were then put aside until a sufficient weight had accumulated to be sold to a silversmith. To combat this, the authorities decided to continue to mint coins at 925-grade silver but decreed that all other silverware had to be produced in the higher grade of 950. This made the 925 clippings impossible to sell and thus put an end to the scam. Unfortunately, the higher-grade silver was more expensive to produce and its extra softness made it more difficult to work, especially in the traditional fine detail of English silver. Consequently, the quality of silverware actually declined and business suffered to the extent that many silversmiths went out of business.

Around the middle of the eighteenth century the government finally accepted that the measure had been counter-productive and they permitted 925-grade silver to be worked again. At the same time the design of coins was changed to the milled edges we know today, so that clipping could be more easily spotted. This measure was successful and ever since that time 950-grade silver has been worked by silversmiths only when specially commissioned by a customer.

The two marks used on Britannia silver are a stamp of Britannia herself and a side profile of a lion's head and shoulders.

Silver plate

Silver plating involves applying a thin layer of silver to the surface of a base metal, usually by a process of electrolysis. There are three types of silver plate: Sheffield plate, EPNS and EPMB. Watch out for the pseudo-hallmarks that some manufacturers of silver-plated items use. These are fancy stamps that could be mistaken for sterling silver hallmarks until you look more closely and see that they are made up of the initial letters indicating the type of silver plate it is.

Sheffield plate is the earliest form of silver plating and is the best quality, as a generous layer of silver is used. The base metal is copper. Items made of Sheffield plate are probably worth about a quarter of those of the same period and similar design made of solid silver but slightly more than EPNS or EPMB.

EPNS stands for Electro-plated Nickel Silver. This method of plating uses a very thin layer of silver applied onto nickel by the process of electrolysis.

EPBM stands for Electro-plated Britannia Metal. It is similar to EPNS but the base metal is of poorer quality.

Chrome

Chromium is a shiny, silvery-coloured metal. Chromium (or 'chrome') plate is often used as a cheaper alternative to silver plate. It was a popular medium for designers working during the 1920s and '30s and even though the material itself has no value, items will find a buyer if they are characteristic of the Art Deco style.

Damage and repairs to silver and silver plate

The method for checking for damage and signs of repair is exactly the same for solid silver and silver-plated items.

Soldering is the most common form of repair. It is easy to spot as it produces a surface that is a duller colour than silver. The places to look for soldering are around the handles, spouts, finials, hinges, etc.

Over-polishing is probably the most common cause of damage. In the case of solid silver, intricate designs can be worn smooth and lose definition or even, in the worst cases, end up with holes in them. The layer of silver on plated items is more susceptible to this kind of wear than solid silver.

Dents are quite commonly caused in solid silver as it is a soft metal. The same goes for EPBM but Sheffield plate and EPNS are more durable. All of them will suffer meltdown if placed directly on a source of heat such as a gas ring.

Replacement parts can be difficult to spot. Always check to see that lids, finials and handles match the rest of the piece or set.

Restoration

In many cases damaged silver can be repaired to a high standard. Having a dent or two knocked out may be worthwhile but, as with all restoration work, the cost of the repair should be balanced against any estimated increase in value. It is by no means unknown for items to go under the hammer for less than it has cost to restore them. If you do decide to have something restored always make sure that the hallmark will not be erased or covered over in the process.

It is quite easy to get a worn EPNS item re-silvered and it should not be too expensive, but ask an expert first whether it's worth it.

Fakes and forgeries

Fake silver is something that purports to be silver but contains no trace of it whatsoever. If you come across anything stamped 'Nevada Silver' or 'Bengal Silver', beware – these pieces are usually made from nickel and have very little value.

There are two common types of forgery where silver is concerned. One is when a silver-plated piece is passed off as solid silver and the other is when it is claimed that a piece is much older than it really is. In both cases the deception is carried out by interfering with the hallmark or adding a bogus one. The usual method is to take a genuine hallmark from a small and therefore relatively low value item and to let it in to the silver-plated or modern silver piece. Luckily, there is a simple test that should expose this fraud: breathe over the hallmark. If it has been 'let-in', then a line will be appear around the hallmark.

Bronze and spelter

Bronze is an alloy of copper with a little tin and often some lead or zinc. It is one of the earliest known alloys, first used around 2500BC. Because it was a much harder material and easier to cast than copper, it was used to produce the weapons and implements of the Bronze Age.

As technology advanced, it was discovered that bronze could be treated to achieve different colours and finishes, mostly in the near-black, brown and green range. If exposed to the elements it will acquire a natural green patina over time as it oxidizes.

Bronze has always been a popular choice for sculpture, ornaments and other items such as coins, but it is expensive to produce. All desirable materials stimulate the search for a cheaper substitute and in the case of bronze it is spelter, which is an impure form of smelted zinc. Since bronze is always going to be worth more than spelter it is important to know how to tell the difference.
Here are a few tips:

- bronze pieces are often much heavier than they appear to be, while spelter pieces are comparatively lightweight
- if a piece has finely worked features, for example if a figure has discernible fingernails, eyelashes, teeth, etc., it is more likely to be bronze, as spelter items

are usually quite crudely cast and will not have delicate detailing

- bronze is smooth and feels cold to the touch while spelter will have a pitted surface and feel warm to the touch
- the colour of bronze looks subtle and even, while spelter looks unnatural and bright

And the final test: turn the piece upside down and gently scratch the surface with the point of a sharp knife. The show-through of bronze is a 'brassy' colour while spelter will reveal an underlying silver colour.

Makers' marks

Most original bronzes will bear the designer's name, usually around the base of the piece, and an actual signature rather than a monogram or stamp will make it more valuable. Some of the most important names to look out for are: Ferdinand Preiss, Pierre Jules Mene, Dimitri Chiparus, Josef Lorenzl, Franz Bergman and Bruno Zach. Preiss is the most sought-after artist of this group and some of his bronzes have been known to fetch as much as £20,000. At the other end of the scale, Lorenzl's spelter sculptures may be picked up for as little as £200.

Ferdinand Preiss (1882–1943) was a German artist, famous for his Art Deco sculptures of radiantly beautiful, healthy-looking females pursuing wholesome activities such as swimming and dancing. His pieces often combine bronze with ivory in a technique known as chryselephantine.

Pierre Jules Mene (1810–79) was a French artist who specialized in realistic sculptures of animals.

Dimitri Chiparus (1888–1950) was a Romanian-born artist who studied and worked in France. He was particularly influenced by the Russian ballet and their jewel-encrusted headdresses and costumes.

Josef Lorenzl (1892–1950) was a very successful Viennese artist who made highly commercial pieces. Typical subjects were women with elongated limbs and slim boyish figures, striking acrobatic or balletic poses.

Franz Bergman (1861–1936) was another Viennese artist specializing in nude or partially clad figures. He often signed his named backwards – 'Namgreb'.

Bruno Zach was a German artist working between the wars whose erotic female figures were drawn from his observation of the cabaret scene in 1930s Berlin.

Decorated bronze

It is quite common for artists to decorate the surface of a bronze, often employing enamelwork techniques, including cold painting, *cloisonné* and *champlevé*. Unfortunately, *cloisonné* and *champlevé* decoration are very easily damaged, and pieces embellished with these techniques are difficult and expensive to repair, so don't expect too much if the enamelling on a bronze is in poor condition.

Cold painting is the decoration of a piece after it has completely cooled. Enamel paints, which are made from coloured pigments added to powdered glass, are usually used in this method.

Cloisonné is a style of decoration that was first developed in China. It is a long and complicated procedure where fine metal wire is soldered to the surface of a piece to create small areas known as '*cloisons*'. The gaps are then filled with enamel and the two elements of the design fused by heat. Watch out for *cloisonné* items that are brightly coloured and stamped 'Made in China' – they are modern and are worth very little.

Champlevé is a similar technique to *cloisonné* but instead of wire being added to create compartments, part of the body of the piece is cut out, and what is left at the original surface level creates the edges of the compartments that are then filled with enamel. As this process is more tricky than *cloisonné*, it is usually reserved for high-quality pieces and so these are generally worth more.

Brass and copper

Copper and brass, which is an alloy of copper and zinc, have long been used for all sorts of practical household objects, as well as ornaments.

Brass

Brass is bright and shiny, malleable, durable and above all affordable. But however much it looks like burnished gold, brassware, sadly, is not very fashionable at the moment, except perhaps for clock cases. The most popular antique brass items are candlesticks but there is also a market for old lamps, warming-pans and horse brasses. Watch out for modern Indian reproductions of these quintessentially English items – they are practically worthless. You may come across brass preserving pans and coal scuttles but copper ones are always going to be worth more (see page 69). Some brassware is marked, like ceramics, with a kite mark (see page 35) and this makes it easier to date.

After polishing your brass, rub it over with olive oil – this will retard tarnishing.

Brass candlesticks The problem with brass candlesticks is that people have been turning them out for centuries, often to the same basic design, and it can be hard to tell the difference between an antique and a reproduction.

The first thing to note is that candlesticks always come in pairs (unless they are chambersticks – see page 68). Whenever you come across a couple, take a good, hard look. People will often try to pass off pairs that don't match so beware of false 'marriages'. Are the two candlesticks identical in every detail? If they are a true pair then the bases should fit perfectly when pushed together. Circular bases are typical of the early part of the nineteenth century and square bases with cut corners became popular later on.

In the days before electricity, when people relied on candles for light in their homes, a candlestick was often fitted with a rod known as a 'pusher'. This protruded into the base and when it was pushed upwards, the stub of candle left in the top would be forced out. Modern candlestick-makers don't usually bother to add a pusher. However, an exception to this general rule are those candlesticks that have a more elaborately worked stem. A barley-sugar twist design, for example, would not allow a rod to be incorporated.

Some manufacturers made their candlesticks in various sizes. One of the most common and popular designs is the 'diamond' series (representing the diamond in a pack of playing cards). They came in 13 sizes, one to represent each card, the largest being the ace, the smallest the 2. The ace and the royal 'cards' fetch the best prices – maybe £150–250 a pair — and they often have their name engraved on the base.

Chambersticks are candlesticks that have a saucer-like base with a looped handle fixed to one side and a small, squat holder for one candle. They were carried about the house – think Wee Willie Winkie – wherever a single light was needed, for example in the bedrooms. A nice Victorian brass chamberstick could be worth as much as £100.

Horse brasses You could be forgiven for thinking that most of the country's old horse brasses have ended up in pubs. You see them everywhere. These small circular or crescent-shaped brass discs mounted in sets of three or five or more on a leather strap or harness are very quaint. It is not really known when or where horse brasses originate but it is known they were used to adorn horses over two thousand years ago, probably as a form of armour to protect the animal in battle. Look for brasses that still have their original leather straps as these are the most collectable.

Lamps Oil lamps and paraffin lamps are also unnecessary in today's world and most people now collect them as ornaments though they would still function if you wanted them to. The standard old-fashioned oil lamp has:

- a brass base containing a well for the oil or paraffin
- a flame adjuster on the side
- a screw top containing the burner
- a glass flue

There are still a lot of brass lamps in circulation. The glass flues were always likely to get broken but if you fitted a new one it would not detract too much from the value.

Warming-pans, like horse brasses, belong to a bygone age. They are obsolete now but they still have a nostalgic appeal. These large circular pans with a hinged lid and a long wooden handle used to be filled with hot coals and then slipped between the sheets to warm a bed. During the day people would often hang them up on the wall and this is what you can do with them today. It is quite common to see them on display in pubs and hotels. Warming-pans engraved with decorative patterns will usually be worth more than plain ones and those with a family crest are the most collectable of all.

Copper

Copper is a reddish-gold coloured metal that was used mainly for kitchenware in the eighteenth and nineteenth centuries. Some cooks still go for copper pans but stainless steel or aluminium is more common in the average kitchen today. With the current fashion for the country kitchen look, though, copper pans are often introduced for that added rustic effect. The most collectable copper items are: kettles, preserving pans, jelly moulds and coal scuttles.

Kettles still seem to be among the most popular items of copperware – there used to be dozens of teashops in England called the Copper Kettle once – so beware of cheap reproductions. Old copper kettles were made from several sections welded together with brass. Look at the back of the main body of the kettle for a distinctive seam. You won't find this on a modern kettle because it will have been cast in one piece. Furthermore, modern kettles are often copper-plated onto brass and you will be able to see this showing through if the piece is worn.

Preserving pans were commonly made in matching sets in different sizes. They were often numbered and some of the wealthier households would have had their name stamped on them. Also known as jam pans, preserving pans are used for making large quantities of jam, marmalade, pickles and chutneys. Even the smallest preserving pan will be much bigger than the average household pan. They were usually lined with tin to prevent the copper from dissolving when it came into contact with the acid that naturally occurs in fruit, and they typically have a cast-iron handle similar to a bucket handle rather than one that sticks out from the side like a saucepan. There is no reason why you should not use old copper pans in

The most common design of copper kettle

your kitchen today as long as the tin lining is intact.

Jelly moulds come in all sorts of wonderful shapes. You have only to look at an old Victorian or Edwardian cookery book to see that they were not just used for desserts as they are today but also served to create wonderful savoury dishes that needed to set, such as salmon in aspic.

Coal scuttles can make attractive items for the home, even if you no longer use coal to heat the living room. For the highest value – up to £150 for a good nineteenth-century example – look for a scuttle shaped like a Roman helmet. It should have the original handle and matching shovel.

Pewter

Pewter is an alloy made from tin mixed with lead or copper. It was commonly used for items of tableware in the Middle Ages, after which time china and glass became more popular for everyday use, though taverns continued to serve ale to their customers in pewter tankards right up to the middle of the nineteenth century.

It does have the advantage of being unbreakable, of course. Pewter has a bright silver appearance to begin with but soon oxidizes and loses its sheen. As a general rule, then, the duller and darker the pewter, the older the piece.

Because pewter has no intrinsic value, collectors are looking for items that are both very old and very rare.

Tankards

The only pewter tankards worth bothering with are those made before 1850, which will fetch two or three times as much as the later ones. Those with a hinged lid will be worth slightly more than those without. Tankards should have two distinctive marks: an excise mark and a touch mark.

Excise marks consist of a set of initials and Roman numerals that refer to the reigning monarch, which will give you a rough idea of the date:

GR or GIV	=	George IV (1820–1830)
WR or WIV	=	William IV (1830–1837)
VR	=	Victoria Regina (1837–1901)
ER or EVII	=	Edward VII (1901–1910)
GR or GV	=	George V (1911–1935)
GRVI	=	George VI (1936–1952)
ERII	=	Elizabeth II (1952–)

Touch marks are the makers' marks, usually a symbol of some kind, that have been registered at the Pewterer's Hall in London.

A Liberty pewter vase designed by Archibald Knox

Glass-bottomed tankards are another viable collecting area. These date back to the Napoleonic Wars at the beginning of the nineteenth century. Around this time less than 5 per cent of sailors in the British Navy had actually volunteered their services and the Navy depended heavily on press gangs to recruit men. These gangs would surreptitiously place a coin in the bottom of the tankard of an unsuspecting lad. Eventually, the coin would be revealed and the unfortunate individual was deemed to have accepted the King's (or Queen's) shilling and so was recruited. This is why glass-bottomed tankards were introduced. The theory was that the outline of the shilling would be clearly visible before the victim had finished his drink and so he could avoid being press-ganged. How effective this was in practice is debatable. The press gangs were not known to dwell on technical niceties and many a lad would awake from a drunken stupor to find himself at sea – literally.

Designer pewter ware

Pewter, which had fallen out of fashion by the end of the nineteenth century, was redis-covered by many designers of the Arts and Crafts movement. They saw it as an honest material that was affordable and attractive. Two manufacturers in particular emerge from this period as the masters of finely crafted pewter ware: WMF and Liberty & Co.

WMF is the Wurttembergische Metallwaren Fabrik, a German company that specialized in the typical Art Nouveau motifs of water nymphs, whiplash and tendrils.

Liberty & Co produced a lot of fashionable pewter ware, including the popular Celtic-inspired 'Tudric' range created by their leading designer, Archibald Knox. (Knox also designed silver jewellery for Liberty's – see page 91 for details of his 'Cymric' range.)

7

Clocks and watches

The first weight-driven mechanical clocks were made in Italy in the first half of the fourteenth century and they were housed in specially built bell towers. These early clocks were usually associated with churches. The oldest surviving example in Britain, which can be found at Salisbury Cathedral, was installed around 1386. Peter Henlein of Nuremberg invented the spring-powered clock in about 1500. He was able to use smaller, lighter weights and so for the first time clocks became a domestic item, though only the wealthy could afford them to begin with.

Clocks

The period from 1660 to 1720 is known as the golden age of clocks and it was a time when clockmakers were at the cutting edge of science and technology, always looking for ways to improve accuracy and reliability.

In 1670 William Clement discovered that a pendulum that was approximately 90 cm (36 inches) long took exactly one second to swing back and forth.

Thomas Tompion (1638–1713) and his contemporary Daniel Quare (1647–1724), both London-based, are the two men whose names always crop up when people talk about fine English clock and watchmakers. Tompion made two clocks for the Royal Greenwich Observatory that only needed winding once a year and he was the first maker to give his pieces a unique serial number.

There are thousands of varieties of clock but most fall into one of the following categories: longcase, bracket, mantel, carriage, public and wall clocks.

Longcase clocks

Commonly known as grandfather clocks, longcase clocks were first made in the 1600s, following the introduction of pendulums to regulate the weight-driven mechanism. The wooden cases are a way of protecting the weights and pendulums so that the time-keeping is as accurate as possible.

Grandfather clocks use two types of weight-driven movement. The simplest has only one weight, which means the clock must be wound up with a key every 30 hours. The second type has two weights and will only need winding once every eight days. As they have slightly more complex movements, these eight-day clocks are deemed to be more collectable.

A clock with just one winding hole will tell the time and nothing more. Strictly speaking, this is known as a 'timepiece', though the term is often used loosely to refer to any instrument that tells the time. If a clock has two winding holes it means that it has a striking mechanism and it will strike on the hour and usually on the half and quarter hour as well.

Dating and valuing a longcase clock

The earliest longcase clocks are quite plain to look at. They have square faces made of brass and some of them have only one hand, which tells the quarter hour. They were very popular in rural areas, where accurate time-keeping was perhaps not important, but urban tastes soon demanded something more sophisticated. The basic square face acquired an arched top in the 1720s and this housed a moon movement or sometimes the maker's name. White painted faces appeared after 1770 and even though they are quite decorative they are not the most desirable.

If you can find a maker's mark on the clock face your research should be straightforward, using reference books. Another useful tip is to look carefully at the case. A longcase clock is, after all, a piece of furniture, so what it looks like will be determined by the design fashions and materials of the day.

The finest clock cases in the eighteenth century were made by specialist cabinet-makers in imported woods such as mahogany, walnut and satinwood. These were the clocks for wealthy clients; people of more modest means made do with plain cases in English oak. The more expensive clock cases were often elaborately carved or had marquetry inlay and some of them were further embellished with brass finials and columns. Clock cases also lent themselves to the style known as *Chinoiserie* that was all the rage at this time, and many of these oriental-inspired painted designs were enriched with gold leaf.

Clock faces

Most clock faces are made from brass, sometimes with silver-plated decoration. Copper was also used, but was not so popular, and this could be painted or enamelled. Some clock face paintings are extremely attractive and the best can be seen as works of art in their own right, enhancing the overall value of the piece. Queen Victoria's love of Scotland started a fashion for Highland scenes and they are a common theme of clock paintings during her reign.

As technology progressed, subsidiary dials started to appear on clock faces. There are three main types – moon dials, date dials and seconds dials – and a clock that has these will generally be worth more than one that doesn't. Best of all is a clock with all three features.

This longcase clock was made in England in the late nineteenth century

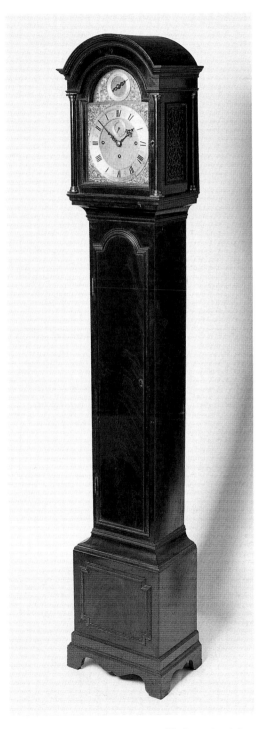

Moon dials are found at the top of the clock face. They show the 29 phases of the moon.

Date dials, also known as calendar dials, show the date number, although they do not refer to the day of the week or the month.

Seconds dials have a single hand that constantly sweeps around, indicating the passing of the seconds.

Damage, restoration and alteration

As in all areas of antiques or collectables, if a piece is not in perfect condition it can lose value. With clocks there are several things you should look out for: general damage to the case, overpainting on the dial, replacement parts and 'marriages'.

General damage to the wooden case of a grandfather clock is hard to avoid as they are heavy objects that are difficult to move around. And because they were expensive to buy at the outset most families held on to them and handed them down through the generations.

The two main scourges of wood are woodworm and damp. In the days before chemical treatments and central heating people often used to cut away the affected part and put a new piece of wood in. This can spell disaster for the value of a clock if the repair looks botched. And if the wood at the base of a longcase clock standing on a damp floor started to rot it was not unknown for owners simply to chop the bottom off to sort the problem out. And the same thing often happened if they wanted to move a clock and found it was too tall to fit – most of them are at least 1.8 m (6 ft). A less drastic remedy was to take the decorative finials off the top of the clock in order to reduce its height but it is sheer vandalism even so.

Overpainting is always a temptation if the numbers on the dial have worn off or if the surface is crazed but it is often done so badly that it would have been better not to do anything at all. Some wear is inevitable with painted faces because of the constant movement of the hands and exposure to changes in temperature.

Replacement parts are a problem because most clocks will need mending at some stage, especially if they are very old. It's all a question of how sympathetically it is done. Obvious signs of poor restoration include filled-in holes or dials with no movement behind them. A clock face is attached to the movement by a series of metal rods. If the face has been replaced you should be able to see the marks left behind by the original rods. But a word of caution: unless you really know what you are doing never dismantle a clock yourself in order to inspect it but take it to an expert.

'Marriages' occur when a clock face is fitted to a case that did not originally belong to it. Such cannibalism is quite common, unfortunately, and you will need to be very observant to spot it. You may get some inkling if the whole piece looks badly proportioned or if there is an unattractive gap between the face and the case. If you do end up with an unfortunate marriage, expect the value to drop.

Bracket clocks

In the mid-seventeenth century it became possible to make clocks with smaller pendulums and so it was no longer necessary for them to have long cases and stand on the floor. Bracket clocks were still heavy enough to need to be hung on a wall securely with a bracket but they did have a handle on top so they were technically portable. Like longcase clocks, they had wooden cases and these were often elaborately decorated according to the fashion of the time. Popular decorative trends included ormolu, which is an extremely ornate technique involving intricate castings of bronze highlighted with real gold (gilding), and boulle, a technique invented by Andrea Charles Boulle (1642–1732) using polished tortoiseshell inlaid with brass in extravagant patterns.

English bracket clocks, especially those made by Thomas Tompion and Daniel Quare, are deservedly highly valued but you could do worse than a German clock made in the late nineteenth century.

A japanned bracket clock made by Thomas Prior of London, *c.*1770

Mantel clocks

Progressing from the bracket clock, mantel clocks were even smaller and were designed to sit on the mantelpiece above a fire (see page 72). As attractive clocks became cheaper to produce most households could afford at least one mantel clock for their living room.

Mantel clocks can be divided into five main categories: ormolu or spelter, black slate, American gingerbread, Napoleon's hat and clock sets.

Ormolu and spelter are similar in appearance but there is an enormous difference in value. The best way to tell the difference is to turn the piece upside down and gently scratch the surface with a sharp knife. Ormolu will show through as a brassy colour whereas spelter will look silvery. Clocks made of both materials were produced in France from around 1750. The cases and faces tended to be quite elaborate though the actual movement inside were not very sophisticated. From around 1830 hand-painted porcelain plaques were incorporated. The best ones were manufactured by the Sèvres porcelain factory and are usually referred to as 'Sèvres panels'. Production of ormolu clocks continued well into the twentieth century. Accurate identification and dating is important as the range of values is very wide indeed. It's always worth unscrewing the chiming bell on the back plate as some manufacturers chose this particular spot to mark their clocks. Clocks made by Japy Frères in Paris are regarded as being among the best of this type.

Black slate was a popular material in the nineteenth century as it was quarried in huge quantities (mostly in Wales) and it could be doctored to look like marble at a fraction of the cost of the real thing. Black slate clocks matched the black slate mantelpieces in many Victorian drawing rooms and were typically fashioned in the Neoclassical style, sometimes like miniature Roman temples, with columns at the front. The cases are normally made of wood overlaid with a thin veneer of slate. Rather unsubtle for modern tastes, and with only basic movements, they are not greatly valued today. If you stumble on one made of green slate rather than black you might fare better as there is definitely a market for these.

American gingerbread clocks were produced in the USA by companies such as the Ansonia Clock Company and were imported into Britain from the 1840s. They get their name from the fact that the decorative front of the clock is very thin, like gingerbread, with the encased movement protruding at the back. Very poor quality movements mean they will never be worth a fortune but a nineteenth-century piece in decent condition could fetch a modest £100–150.

Napoleon's hat clocks were mass-produced from about 1920 onwards. Cheap, cheerful, and with plywood cases, they are so common that they are not worth much, maybe £60–100 for a good one made by Smiths in England in the 1930s. But they have a reputation for reliable timekeeping and usually strike the quarter and half hours, with a full Westminster chime (which imitates Big Ben) on the hour.

Clock sets date from around 1830 and are sometimes referred to as 'clock garnitures'. They consist of a clock with two sidepieces, which could be a pair of vases, candlesticks or dishes known as *tazzas* or 'comports'. A *tazza* (from the Italian for 'cup') was the name of a shallow drinking vessel used in Italy in the sixteenth and seventeenth centuries. The word was later applied to any flat dish supported on a central stem.

The clocks in these sets were usually made of cheap spelter or black slate but you might be fortunate enough to come across an ormolu one by a renowned French maker like Japy or Cailland, in which case it could be worth several thousand pounds.

Carriage clocks

By the mid-eighteenth century it was possible to buy a clock that was genuinely portable. This was a wonderful innovation for travellers, who could now keep track of the time during the course of a journey. The carriage clock is believed to have been invented by Abraham-Louis Breguet (1747–1823). The standard design is square, with four bevelled glass panels encased in a brass frame with a brass handle on top. Early examples had a leather carrying case with a panel at the front that could be moved to reveal the clock face.

Carriage clocks do not have a pendulum (which would not function in a clock that was moving) but instead have what is known as a 'platform' movement, which is laid horizontally and sits on a platform. A very useful feature of some carriage clocks, and one that will add value, is a repeater. You press a button on top of the case to get the clock to 'repeat' its last series of chimes. This gives you the time to the nearest quarter hour. Some also have an alarm function.

For the highest value, look for a well-known maker, such as Breguet, or upmarket retailers

A French carriage clock and its leather carrying case made by Henri Jacot around 1890

like Asprey and Garrard, who sometimes had their names added to the clocks they sold. You could expect to get around £500 for a middle of the range carriage clock but it is also worth knowing that:

- English carriage clocks are usually more valuable than French ones
- a carriage clock with its original carrying case is highly desirable
- an alarm, a repeater and subsidiary dials will all add value

Public clocks

In 1797 the government imposed a tax on privately owned clocks and watches and this had quite an effect: it encouraged the spread of clocks in public places. These came in two basic designs: the so-called 'Act of Parliament' clock and the dial clock.

Act of Parliament clocks acquired their name as a direct consequence of the new tax. They are easily identified by their very large wooden faces and tall wooden cases, which are about 90 cm (36 inches) high. Early versions had no glass over the dial – this was introduced in around 1830. Because they represent a curious episode in English history, Act of Parliament clocks will always find a buyer willing to pay perhaps more than £5000, even if the piece is not in good condition and requires restoration.

Dial clocks are the familiar round-faced clocks that were once a feature of every railway station and civic building in the country. They were usually made of mahogany and had clear white dials with Roman numerals painted in black. It is a classic design that never seemed to date until the digital revolution came along and literally changed the face of the modern clock.

There were two types of coil-spring movement used in the dial clock: the standard, straight-coiled spring and the 'fusee' type, recognizable by its cone shape. Clocks with a fusee movement are the more collectable as they are more accurate timekeepers.

Nostalgia will always ensure the market for a dial clock, especially if it has local significance in the shape of a maker's name or a place name. And you can always predict an above-average price for clocks associated with the railways.

Wall clocks

Wall clocks come in a variety of shapes and designs. From about 1800 factories in Vienna produced wall clocks known as regulators. The movements in these clocks were extremely accurate, though the design was basic, lacking any frivolous accessories such as chimes. The purpose of a regulator was to serve as a 'master' clock against which all other clocks, for example in a household or a hotel, could be set, hence their name.

In the mid-nineteenth century Viennese regulators were being copied in Germany, but not to such a high a standard. It is quite useful to be able to spot the difference because a genuine Vienna regulator will be worth £1000 or more, which is around twice as much as a German copy.

Vienna regulators have plain cases, but in high-quality wood, They have only one winding hole. They are weight-driven and have a grid iron pendulum. A grid iron pendulum is made from rods of steel and brass combined. These metals have different coefficients of expansion and this limits the effects of temperature changes, resulting in very accurate timekeeping.

Vienna-style German reproductions are often made to quite elaborate designs, typically with eagle carvings on top. They have two or three winding holes. They are spring-driven and have a wooden pendulum with a brass weight.

American wall clocks began to appear in Britain in around 1850. They usually contain low-quality movements in poorly made cases and are unlikely to go beyond £100 at auction, maybe a bit more if they are hand-painted, when they become more of a novelty. The decorators used a technique known as *verre églomisé* in which the image is painted back to front on the inside of the glass so that it appears the right way round when you look at it. Look out for a typical American landscape.

Watches

Watches fall into two broad categories: pocket watches and wristwatches.

Pocket watches first made an appearance in the late 1600s and they were originally made by locksmiths and blacksmiths because these were the people who knew how to make the coiled spring that drove the mechanism.

As technology advanced, and watches became more sophisticated and decorative, clockmakers and silversmiths took over, turning watchmaking into a specialist trade. By the end of the eighteenth century most gentlemen owned a gold or silver pocket watch, though they were far too expensive for the ordinary man.

The first wristwatches were made in the early 1900s and they were so practical that soon the pocket watch was rendered completely obsolete. They were still regarded as a purchase for special occasions until the 1960s, when plastic watches made in the Far East turned them into a disposable fashion accessory. That is not to say that all modern watches are cheap – in 1999 in New York the 'Supercomplication', a Patek Phillipe men's wristwatch, sold at auction for more than £6.8 million!

Pocket watches

The important centres for early pocket watches were Nuremberg, Flanders and Burgundy. However, throughout the nineteenth century the best pocket watches were made in Britain. Because of this, many of the top continental craftsmen came to work here – further improving the quality of the watches.

The pocket watch was originally designed to fit into the pocket of a gentleman's waistcoat. The early designs did not have a chain – this idea became popular after Prince Albert first wore one in 1845. After this it became the fashion to place the watch in the pocket on one side of the waistcoat and have the chain stretched across the chest and secured by means of a T-bar pushed through the buttonhole on the pocket on the other side of the waistcoat. These became known as 'Albert chains'.

As well as keeping the watch safe and making it easier for the wearer to pull it out of his pocket, a chain added status. It was a sign of wealth and some men who could not afford a watch would just wear a chain to give the impression of being well-to-do.

Watch keys were easily lost when they were kept separate so eventually they were designed to be attached to the T-bar end of the chain, sometimes alongside a vesta case for matches. Today people sometimes wear watch chains like a necklace or bracelet, with the watch key or a seal attached.

Ladies' pocket watches were introduced towards the end of the nineteenth century. They were smaller than the men's and the cases were often set with jewels and the faces enamelled. As ladies tended not to wear waistcoats, they hung their watches from the lapel of their jackets on a chain, which became known as an 'Albertina' guard chain or 'granny chain'.

Valuing

Since the early eighteenth century the pocket watch has gone through many developments. Generally speaking, as with most antiques, the earlier the piece, the higher the value, but there are other factors at play, including: the metal used for the case, the maker's reputation and the type and condition of the piece.

Age

1700–1800 Watches made in Britain in the eighteenth century were quite bulky and usually very plain while those from continental Europe were often decorated with jewels or enamel. Some of the watches were chain-driven and in these cases the tiny metal chains are visible in the movement. Some have two keyholes in the back, one for winding the hands, the other for winding the movement; and others, like many longcase clocks of this period, have only one hand.

1800–1900 By the beginning of the nineteenth century watch cases had started to become slimmer and more decorative, and cogs and wheels were replacing the old chain mechanism. Subsidiary dials were a new feature that quickly gained popularity, though watches with chimes did not really catch on. From around 1870 most watches were screw-wound and no longer needed keys.

1900–1920 The introduction of the first wristwatch in the 1900s spelt the end of the pocket watch and production dramatically decreased after about 1920.

An enamel-faced ladies' pocket watch, *c.*1890

Watch cases

All pocket watch cases were made of metal, usually silver, gold, rolled gold or platinum. At the cheaper end of the scale gunmetal was used. Obviously, the type of metal used for the case bears heavily on the value of a watch. Even irreparable non-working watches made of platinum, gold or silver will at least have a bullion value. British watches will often have a hallmark, usually inside the back plate, which will help you to date it. Decoration on a watch case, for example the use of precious stones or enamelwork, will often increase its value.

Makers

The watchmaker's name will always influence the value of a watch. Those to look out for include: Thomas Tompion and Daniel Quare in the late seventeenth and early eighteenth centuries; Abraham-Louis Breguet in the late eighteenth and early nineteenth centuries; Patek Philippe, Omega, Longines, Cartier and Waltham from the middle of the nineteenth century to the present day; and Rolex from the 1900s onwards.

Pocket watch types

The main types of pocket watch are: pair-cased, full hunter and demi hunter, open-faced, military and ladies'.

Pair-cased pocket watches are the earliest type of pocket watch and they were produced from the middle of the seventeenth century until about 1870. They have a removable outer case, usually in a single type of metal, that is designed to give added protection. The finest examples are those made by Tompion, which are easily worth £10,000 or more. Quare and Breguet are less expensive but still pricy at anything up to £3000 or so.

Open-faced pocket watches are the most common type. They have a white painted dial, with a glass cover held in a metal ring known as a bezel.

Full hunter and demi hunter pocket watches came in in the 1840s and they got their name because people originally wore them when they went foxhunting. Full hunters have a solid hinged cover rather than a glass one over the face. A demi hunter, also known as a half hunter, has a hinged cover too but its main distinguishing features are a convex glass centrepiece and the repetition of the roman numerals on the cover. These allow you to tell the time at a glance without opening the watch – very handy when you are out riding. Typically made in rolled gold, silver and 9ct or 18ct gold, prices can range from £25 to £350 or more. Demi hunters are deemed to be more attractive than full hunters and could be worth twice as much.

Military pocket watches are usually made of gunmetal, which is a combination of copper and tin, blue-grey in colour. A cheap and durable material, it was also plentiful, being a common by-product from the manufacture of guns, and the watches were standard army issue (for officers only!) in the nineteenth and early twentieth centuries, especially during wartime. Average prices are around £50 unless there is a proven regimental connection or the watch bears a well-known maker's name.

Ladies' pocket watches are smaller, more decorative versions of open-faced and full and demi hunter watches. Being smaller than a man's watch does not affect their value, which depends on factors other than size, such as age and condition, and all the major watchmakers produced them.

Complex movements

The term 'complex movement' refers to any feature that is additional to the basic time-telling function of a watch. These features might include: chronographs, chronometers, perpetual calendars, moon phases and world time.

A chronograph is a watch that also includes a stopwatch.

A chronometer is a highly complex movement that keeps accurate time under any condition, including changes in atmospheric pressure, temperature or movement. It was the invention of the chronometer that enabled longitude to be determined at sea, vastly increasing the accuracy of navigation.

A perpetual calendar shows the date of the month and automatically allows for the different number of days in each month.

A moon phase shows the 29 phases of the moon.

World time is a small dial on the watch face set to the time on a different longitude, such as New York or Sydney.

Pocket watch accessories

There was a fair bit of paraphernalia associated with wearing a pocket watch in the old days and many of these accessories are now worth collecting separately. As well as watch chains, there was a whole variety of other things that wearers could hang from them, including: fobs, keys, vesta cases and chatelaines.

Watch chains can be attractive even when there is no longer a watch to go with them. They are usually made of 9ct gold or silver and some people wear them as necklaces or bracelets. A gold chain should have a carat mark stamped on each individual link, so always check to make sure that every part of it is solid and hasn't been patched with rolled or plated gold. The guard chains or granny chains that were made for ladies' pocket watches typically have uniform, box-shaped links and they are much longer than the Albert chains made for gentlemen's watches.

Fobs are small ornaments made to hang from a watch chain. There are many different designs but most take the form of two semi-precious stones, bloodstone and agate being a popular combination, that swivel to give the wearer a choice of which colour to display. Fobs occasionally incorporate useful accessories, such as a compass or a seal carved with the owner's monogram.

Keys are easily lost, but as those that were made for the old pocket watches were not unique, finding a replacement if you need one shouldn't be too difficult. On the other hand, if you have a key without a watch it is always worth having it valued because there is a market for the best examples, some of which are beautifully made and very attractive.

Vesta cases were made in the nineteenth century for the safekeeping of matches (vestas) in the days before lighters were invented. They have a hinged lid and a distinctive ridge on one edge, which is where you struck the match to get a light. Various metals were used in their manufacture, the most popular being silver, in which case the items will have a hallmark. Although some vesta cases are finely crafted, with artistic engravings or enamelled decoration, many were made as cheap novelty items. As a reminder of the days when smoking was regarded as a harmless activity they are great fun to collect. The price range is enormous – from less than £100 to several thousand pounds.

Chatelaines, in the context of pocket watch chains (there are other meanings associated with the term), are clasps or pendants designed to carry a selection of useful little items, such as scissors and keys, as well as decorative trinkets.

Wristwatches

It is believed that Louis-François Cartier invented the first wristwatch in 1907 after a friend of his, who was an airship pilot, told him how awkward it was to check the time with a pocket watch whilst at the controls. And for a similar reason, the military started issuing wristwatches as soon as the technology allowed. British officers certainly had them during the First World War.

Military issue wristwatches are usually made of gunmetal or stainless steel, coupled with the best quality movements to ensure accuracy. These watches are an exception to the general rule that cheap cases house an inferior movement. (Inferior movements are machine-made from cheap materials and are often unsigned, although they may be stamped with the country of origin. They are less accurate than hand-made movements, which are made using high-quality materials and clearly stamped with the maker's mark.)

Military issue wristwatches also have a distinctive arrow pointing upwards, sometimes with a serial number stamped underneath. Look for this mark either on the back of the case, on the outside, or on the dial. (The maker's name will be found inside the watch.) The dials are almost always black with luminous painted dots or dashes to represent every five minutes. The following marks and serial numbers will help you with identification:

6B: made for the RAF
W10: made for the Women's Land Army
www: waterproof wristwatch

Condition

As usual, condition is an important element of valuation with watches. If the screw-wind is

This 18-carat Omega wristwatch with complex movement (a stopwatch) was made in the 1930s

or balance wheel may be defective. Never use force and if in doubt always consult a professional watch repairer. In many cases, a simple clean or basic repair is all that is needed. Common types of damage that can easily be fixed include mending or replacing hands, winders, hanging hooks and the glass.

Some damage is not so easily repaired and will be detrimental to the value of a watch, such as:

- cracks to the enamel dial
- chipped enamel
- water damage, especially rust
- broken hinges
- broken main springs

tight on a pocket watch it may have been over-wound. If you are able to turn the screw but cannot get the watch to go, it is worth checking the movement inside. Carefully open the back and then gently rock the watch from side to side; if the circular hair spring moves back and forth, it is probably repairable; if it does not move, the hair spring

Always get an estimate of the cost before getting a repair done – you may find it won't seem worth it. In these cases if you don't want to keep the watch for sentimental reasons you could ask the watch repairer if it has a bullion value or whether it is worth anything for its spare parts.

8

Jewellery

When you look at a piece of jewellery can you tell whether it is expensive or cheap? Are the materials real or fake? You can adorn yourself with anything, from the most costly gold right down to a piece of shell washed up on the beach. You can use precious stones – diamonds, rubies, sapphires and emeralds – or semi-precious stones, such as amethysts, garnets and opals. You can use coloured glass cut to look like expensive gems. Natural or synthetic, decorated or plain, the choice is yours. If you have some jewellery to sell the first step to finding out how much it is worth is to establish what it is made of.

The three most common metals used for high-quality jewellery are platinum, gold and silver. Known as the precious metals, they will always have a bullion value, which means that they will always be worth something regardless of what they have been fashioned into.

Platinum

Platinum is a silvery-coloured metal occurring naturally, typically as small grains within nickel ore. One of the reasons that it is so highly regarded is that it is quite difficult to mine and extract. In addition, it is also much harder than gold, having a higher melting point, and this makes it the most valuable metal of all.

The Spanish conquistadors first brought platinum to Europe from South America in the sixteenth century.

Although there is no reason apart from the expense why a piece should not be made entirely from platinum, it is more commonly used for setting high-quality stones into high carat gold jewellery. There are two reasons for this: firstly, the stones are more secure in the harder platinum setting, and secondly, most stones, especially diamonds, appear brighter when offset against a platinum background. Stones set in gold often take on a dull yellowish hue, which is usually considered less attractive than the sparkling effect that platinum creates.

If you find it difficult to distinguish platinum from silver, simply look for the abbreviation 'plat' that should be stamped somewhere on the piece.

Gold

Gold has always been a commodity of serious investment as it usefully combines small bulk with high value. And in some countries, when the economic climate is uncertain, gold can seem like a safer alternative to money in the bank.

Some people keep modern gold coins purely for their bullion value and have no interest in them otherwise. Even gold jewellery in really bad condition has some re-sale value. If you have any gold that is arguably not worth keeping, then take the items to a reputable jeweller and ask for a price. You will probably find someone who is willing to buy small quantities of scrap gold in order to melt it down or to use it to repair other pieces.

The value of gold moves with the stock market so buying and selling prices will change every day. For the connoisseur of fine jewellery, bullion value is not the point, of course, for while many a piece is literally worth its weight in gold, what everyone is looking for is that rare beauty in a piece that will turn something valuable into something priceless.

Gold remains the most popular of the three precious metals and it comes in a variety of purities and colours. As it is an extremely soft metal, other metals, such as silver or copper (or sometimes a mixture of the two), are often added to it to make it more durable. Pure gold is classified as 24 carat but when it is combined with other metals the carat rating drops, so the less gold there is in the mix the lower the carat. An expert can tell the carat just by handling an item but for those with less experience the hallmark is the key, as by law the quality of all gold must be shown.

On modern pieces you may notice that the hallmark is indicated not with a carat number, such as 9ct, but as a three-digit number, such as 375. A new system was introduced in Britain in 1975 to show what percentage of gold a piece contains. So 100 per cent pure gold, 24ct, is represented by 1000 at one end of the scale, while 9ct gold at the other end would be marked 375, indicating that it contains 375 parts per 1000 gold. This innovation brings the marking of gold in line with that used for silver (see page 60). Occasionally you may find a gold hallmark that combines the two systems, e.g. 9.375.

Carat ratings for gold

9ct (375) This is the lowest carat rating used for gold. It has a purity of 9 parts gold to 15 parts (375 per 1000) other metals and this makes it the hardest gold in common use. Most British designers choose 9ct gold for good-quality dress or costume jewellery. Until fairly recently precious stones were never set into anything below 14ct, so if you have a 9ct piece of jewellery that you know to be old you can be fairly confident that the stones will not be worth very much.

14ct (585) This quality of gold is popular in continental Europe and the USA. Its ratio is 14 parts gold to 10 parts (585 per 1000) other metals. If you come across a gold piece stamped 'kt' there is a fair chance that it is from America, where the letters stand for 'karat', an alternative spelling of 'carat'. It is a good idea to avoid wearing two different carats of gold next to each other, for example two rings on the same finger, as the harder gold piece can sometimes make the softer one wear thin.

15ct This carat has not been used in Britain since 1932.

18ct (750) At 18 parts gold to 6 parts (750 per 1000) other metals, this is the most usual mix that jewellery-makers select when they want to create an expensive piece using precious stones.

22ct (916) It is generally felt that this quality – 22 parts gold to 2 parts (916 per 1000) other metals – is too soft to use successfully as a setting for precious stones as there would be a high risk of them wearing loose and falling out of the piece. Plain wedding rings are typically fashioned from 22ct gold.

Additional markings

As well as the carat rating, the following marks are sometimes found on gold.

Assay marks are sometimes found on gold items and these enable you to date a piece in exactly the same way as silver (see page 60 for an explanation of how to date hallmarks).

Makers' marks are a set of identifying initials that some makers stamp on their gold pieces. These marks will generally have little bearing on value, unless the maker has acquired an exceptional reputation for so-called 'designer' jewellery.

Colour variations

When pure gold is mixed with other metals it will have an effect on the colour.

Yellow gold is the result of adding silver and copper to gold and is one of the most common forms.

Rose gold is the result when just copper on its own it added to gold, producing a reddish-gold colour.

White gold is the most expensive combination of all and is created when gold is mixed with platinum or silver or nickel and zinc. It looks like silver but you can tell the difference by checking the hallmark.

All that glitters …

Because gold is so desirable it is not surprising that people have always looked for cheaper substitutes. The three most common gold imitators are pinchbeck, rolled gold and gold plate, and while they can all look very much like the real thing they are worth a mere fraction, so don't be deceived. If you are unsure, ask a jeweller to check on the metal using jeweller's acid.

If you were to take four 'gold' items, such as a rope brooch, all made in, say, 1890, then the solid gold one would be worth £200–300 while the pinchbeck piece would probably be worth £60–100. There's not much to choose between the other two and they really are the poor relations – you would be lucky to realize more than £20 or so for an old rolled gold or gold plate rope brooch, even though it might be over a hundred years old.

Pinchbeck takes its name from the man who allegedly first discovered that mixing zinc and copper produces a shiny, gold-looking alloy that is even harder than 9ct gold. Christopher Pinchbeck was a clock and watchmaker working in London and when he died in 1732 it is said that his formula for this false gold died with him. His name now also stands for anything that is tawdry or fake. Pinchbeck jewellery from the early eighteenth century is very collectable indeed and even pieces from the late Victorian era have a respectable value today. It does not qualify for a hallmark so you may need an expert to help you to identify it.

Rolled gold, unlike pinchbeck, does at least have some gold content, though never very much. It is created by fusing sheets of gold to the surface of copper, then rolling it out, a bit like pastry, to the desired thickness. This is a perfectly legitimate way of producing something that looks like solid gold – as long as it is stamped with the letters 'rg' and not passed off as something it isn't. One thing to look for on old pieces are the telltale reddish patches that appear when the gold wears off, revealing the underlying copper base.

Gold plate is produced by transferring gold onto the surface of a base metal such as nickel by electrolysis. It is the gold equivalent of silver plate or EPNS (see page 64). As with rolled gold, the surface tends to wear off after a while and then the base metal will show through. Rolled gold pieces are sometimes stamped with a carat number followed by the letters 'gp'.

Silver

Silver has always been a popular choice for making jewellery as it is relatively easy to work with and is more affordable than gold. It would be unusual to find it as a setting for precious stones, so silver pieces are unlikely to fetch much.

Expect to see prices ranging from £100–250 for an early twentieth-century brooch, for example, even one made by such well-known and important silversmiths and designers as Georg Jensen, Murrle, Bennett & Co, Charles Horner or Archibald Knox.

Georg Jensen (1866–1935) was a Danish designer working in the Art Nouveau and Art Deco styles, who specialized in silver jewellery with a nautical theme. He sometimes used semi-precious stones in his work. He usually stamped his pieces with his initials or, in some cases, his full name.

Murrle, Bennett & Co was a British company that made simple, affordable jewellery, with geometric designs. They are especially known for using turquoises. Their work is stamped MB&Co.

Charles Horner (1837–96) was a British silversmith who worked for Liberty & Co. His designs are quite austere. They incorporate plain geometric shapes and are often decorated with enamel. His work is stamped with his initials.

Archibald Knox (1864–1933) was also a designer for Liberty's, specializing in Art Nouveau and Arts and Crafts jewellery. His work is not stamped with his initials but those of Liberty & Co, 'L & C', and the design name 'Cymric'.

Gemstones

Gemstones can be the most valuable part of a piece of jewellery so it is important to be able to identify them. This is not always easy as they all have their cheap imitations.

And old wives' tales abound, especially the one that says that only a real diamond can score the surface of a piece of glass. Believe me, this is not true – another piece of glass would do the job just as well. Natural gemstones are graded either as precious stones or semi-precious stones.

Precious stones

There are four main precious stones – diamonds, rubies, sapphires and emeralds – and their value is dependent on four factors, known as the four C's: carat, clarity, colour and cut.

Diamonds

A diamond is a crystallized form of the mineral carbon, formed by great heat and pressure under the earth's surface. Diamonds are the most prized of all gemstones, although they are quite unimpressive in their natural state, only achieving their sparkle or brilliance when they have been professionally cut and polished.

Carat Diamond size is measured in carats (weight). It is not necessary to remove the stone from its setting to weigh it as the weight can be estimated by using a diamond gauge. Diamonds are precision cut and taper to a point. When the largest surface is measured in a diamond gauge the weight

can be calculated. Rest your stone over the circles and find the one that is the closest fit to the widest part of the stone. You can then cross-reference this to the grid for an approximate value of an average quality, second-hand stone. For a more accurate valuation you should consult a jeweller. It should be noted that two 0.5ct diamonds will not be worth as much as a 1ct stone.

Clarity Many diamonds have naturally occurring imperfections; for example, they may contain specks of carbon that have not crystallized or they may have tiny cracks (known as inclusions) in them. Everyone is looking for the perfect, flawless stone and as these faults reduce the clarity of a diamond they make it less desirable.

Cut There are many types of diamond cut but the most popular are: rose, old, brilliant and baguette. The brilliant cut diamond, although the most recent style of cut, is the most valuable as it shows the diamond off to its best.

Colour Diamonds are naturally colourless but there have been times when it was fashionable to heat-treat them to give them colour. These are known as 'fancy' diamonds and they are less valuable than untreated stones.

Diamond cuts and gauge

Six popular diamond cuts are shown below. To deterimine the carat rating of a diamond, see which of the circles in the diamond gauge at the bottom of the page it most closely fits. (The values are very approximate!)

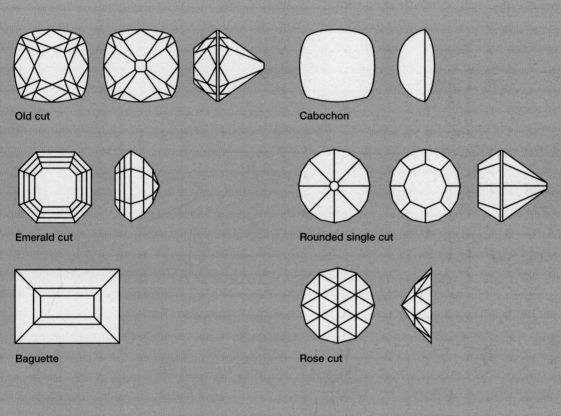

Old cut

Cabochon

Emerald cut

Rounded single cut

Baguette

Rose cut

Diamond gauge

Carats	0.01	0.02	0.05	0.10	0.20	0.25	0.50	0.75	1.00	2.00	4.00
Value (£)	4	6	10	30	80	200	450	700	1000	8000	20,000

Rubies

Rubies are found within the mineral family of corundum and are composed of the two softest elements: aluminium and oxygen. They get their red colour from the chromium in the mix. Most rubies come from Myanmar (Burma) but they are also mined in Kenya, Thailand, Cambodia and Sri Lanka.

Sapphires

Sapphires are also from the corundum family. The word is Hebrew for 'beautiful' and legend has it that Moses returned from Mount Sinai with carved sapphire tablets. Like rubies, sapphires can be artificially produced using a powder of the same chemical composition. It is fascinating how sapphires can change colour according to the light, turning a greeny-blue in sunlight or a reddish-purple in artificial light. Most people expect sapphires to be blue, which they often are, but they come in a variety of other colours too:

Purple The richer colours in the violet blue to purple range tend to be found in sapphires mined in Africa, while the paler pastel colours are more characteristic of stones found in Sri Lanka.

Pink Sometimes referred to as 'Ceylon Sapphires', pink sapphires are the rarest of all and are considered the best in the world. The pink hue can have hints of yellow and red with flashes of orange.

Yellow Sapphires can occur in a fairly wide range of yellow shades, from quite pale to quite dark, and the colour comes from the iron content in the stone. Yellow sapphires are commonly found in Australia.

Green Green sapphires can be quite intense in colour, though they are often yellow underneath, and they are the least desirable.

Emeralds

Emeralds are a green-coloured stone, set into jewellery from ancient times in several locations. Legend has it that the Roman Emperor Nero watched the gladiators though emerald spectacles. Cleopatra had her own emerald mines and the Incas worshipped emeralds. Some of the most precious emeralds in the world are reputed to lie in shipwrecks at the bottom of the ocean after being stolen by the Spaniards (in around 1500).

Emeralds are quite durable but if they are knocked on a hard surface they can fracture. They can be cleaned professionally with some acids and cedar wood oil but cleaning them yourself in warm soapy water and a soft cloth is sufficient.

Semi-precious stones

Any natural mineral that has been mined, cut and polished for decorative purposes can be termed a semi-precious stone. There are hundreds of different ones and some are obviously more prized than others because they are rare or especially beautiful. Popular semi-precious stones used in jewellery-making include jet, amethysts, bloodstones, garnets, marcasite and opals.

Jet

Jet is black and it looks like coal – which is exactly what it is. It is extremely hard and jewellers always polish it well to give it its characteristic glass-like sheen. The best jet, known as Whitby jet, is mined off the coast of North Yorkshire. Although it is mostly

Birthstone quiz

Below is a list of the 12 birthstones, their colours and meanings, but they are in the wrong order – can you sort them out? (The answers are on page 141.)

Month	Stone	Colour	Meaning
	amethyst	blue	clear thinking
	bloodstone or aquamarine	blueish-green	constancy
	diamond	cream	contentment
	emerald	green	courage
	garnet	green or red or blue	fidelity
	opal or tourmaline	light green	health and longevity
	pearl or moonstone or alexandrite	multi-coloured	hope
	ruby	orange or brown	innocence
	sapphire	purple	love and success
	sardonyx or peridot	red	married happiness
	topaz	deep red	prosperity
	turquoise or lapis lazuli	white or clear	sincerity
January			
February			
March			
April			
May			
June			
July			
August			
September			
October			
November			
December			

Amethyst set in a ring

Garnets

Garnets are transparent burgundy-red gemstones. Take care not to confuse them with rubies – they can look similar because of their colour. The name 'garnet' comes from the Latin word 'granatum', meaning 'pomegranate'.

Marcasite

This is made from highly polished pyrite, which is greyish-black in colour.

Opals

Opals are often multi-coloured, usually a mixture of greens, blues and oranges. They are made up of layers of silica gel that has accumulated over millions of years. The word 'opal' is Latin for 'precious stone'.

used for mourning jewellery (see page 99), sailors and fishermen traditionally believe that it brings good luck. It is said that Captain James Cook always took a piece of jet with him on his voyages.

Amethysts

Amethysts were extremely rare until 1760, when a large deposit was discovered in South America. Iron accounts for their natural purple colour but when they are heat-treated the stones turn bright yellow. After this process the material is known as citrine and the colour change is permanent and irreversible.

Bloodstones

These are non-transparent, predominantly green stones with red specks or spots. They are often selected for men's jewellery as the colour green is said to represent wealth, money and business.

Costume jewellery

People who own expensive jewellery have always had to be security conscious. They often keep their best pieces locked away in safety deposit boxes most of the time. Costume jewellery was initially a response to this state of affairs and women would have copies made of their real jewellery so that they could take it with them when travelling and wear it in public without the fear of being robbed.

Costume jewellery is not generally worth very much but there is one area where collectors are beginning to take an interest. Brooches and necklaces by fashionable twentieth-century designers such as Trifari, Miriam Haskell, Christian Dior and Schiaparelli can be picked up for reasonable prices – maybe £50 or £100 or £150 – and are likely to appreciate in value.

Organic materials

Virtually anything can be turned into jewellery and designers have always looked to organic materials to serve their creative imaginations.

In the past they have used items straight from nature, such as pearls, mother-of-pearl, amber, coral and tortoiseshell, but conservationists now warn that these should no longer be plundered from the earth and sea, so artificial alternatives have become more acceptable.

Pearls

Pearls begin life as foreign objects, such as pieces of shell, that become lodged inside a living oyster. In order to protect itself, the oyster secretes a smooth, hard substance called nacre and gradually encases the irritant, eventually forming a hardened sphere. Not every living oyster produces a pearl – unless it is farmed, when the deliberate implantation of alien material produces a near perfect specimen every time. And this is how, with a trained eye, you can tell a cultured pearl from the real thing: a string of cultured pearls will look unnaturally uniform – exactly the same shape and exactly the same colour – while real pearls, being slightly misshapen and varied in colour because they are produced by accident, will display subtle differences. You can expect a real pearl necklace to be worth ten times as much as one made of cultured pearls.

Amber

Amber is fossilized resin from pine trees and is usually red, orange or yellow in colour. People are fascinated by the fact that insects that lived millions of years ago can end up being trapped in amber and because it is a translucent material it is sometimes possible to see these tiny embedded creatures in perfect profile.

Coloured glass and plastic are commonly used to imitate amber and there are one or two things you can do to tell the difference. Real amber feels slightly soft and warm rather than hard and cool. It is not very brittle and it doesn't chip or scratch easily. If you rub it with a soft cloth, creating a fair amount of friction, you should find that you can get a piece of tissue paper to stick to it. You won't be able to do this with a piece of coloured glass or plastic. Plastic amber has a visible seam.

Coral

Coral is a hard organic substance formed from the skeletons of marine polyps. It is usually pinky red or orange. It is believed that coral had powers to ward off evil spirits and was therefore commonly used to fashion babies' rattles.

Tortoiseshell

From the shell of a sea turtle rather than a tortoise, tortoiseshell was popular with the Victorians, who admired its smooth properties, dark yellowish-brown colours and mottled appearance. They fashioned it into little boxes, combs and hairbrushes. Nineteenth-century designers developed a decorative technique known as *piqué*, in which silver or gold was inlaid into a piece of tortoiseshell.

Sentimental jewellery

Although jewellery has always been dictated by fashion, much of it has a sentimental purpose and some of it conveys symbolic meaning. When you consider life's most important milestones and rituals you can be sure that someone has thought of a way of making an item of jewellery to match.

Common life-events would include birth, courtship, betrothal, matrimony and death, and popular themes or sentiments would signify things such as love, grief, religious belief, luck and superstition.

Love, courtship and marriage

Heart-shaped jewellery symbolizes love. Items such as heart-shaped locket pendants have always been popular for sentimental keepsakes such as a lock of hair or a picture of someone one wants to remember.

A lovebird with a flower– usually a forget-me-not – in its beak also symbolizes true love and stands for the bearer of good news. These were popular motifs during both the First and Second World Wars when people were parted from one another.

The image of cupid, a winged messenger sent from the gods to make people fall in love when his arrow pierces their hearts is another popular romantic symbol.

The tradition of the diamond engagement ring is not all that old, though betrothal rings have a long history in most European societies, symbolizing unity, perfection and eternity.

The tradition of wearing the engagement and wedding rings on the third finger of the left hand derives from Roman times. This particular finger was believed to contain the *vena amoris* – the 'vein of love' – and it was

believed that this vein led directly to the heart.

One of the most famous types of courtship ring is the Claddagh ring, believed to have originated some 400 years ago in the fishing village of Claddagh, which overlooks Galway Bay in Ireland. The ring has two hands clasping a heart with a crown above, and the way it is worn conveys a message Worn on the right hand with the heart upside down means you are unattached. Worn with the heart the right way up means you are courting but open to offers! Worn the right way up on the left hand means you are betrothed.

The wedding band has been used since at least the Roman times. It is believed that in the twelfth century Pope Innocent III decided that weddings should take place in church and that rings should be made part of the marriage ceremony. A wedding band is the perfect symbol of unity, being an unbroken circle that has no beginning and no end.

It is quite uncommon to find second-hand wedding rings for sale, as most people want something new to start them off in married life. Most jewellers will offer the bullion value but no more.

Posy rings are wedding bands that have an inscription on the inside.

Eternity rings are sometimes referred to as 'best' wedding rings as they are really just wedding rings set with precious stones. They are often bought by a husband as an expression of his continued love for his wife on a wedding anniversary or when their children are born. Diamonds are the most popular stone for eternity rings but others may be chosen, for example a ruby to celebrate a fortieth wedding anniversary.

The most common type of eternity ring is the half-eternity, so called because the stones only go halfway round the ring. Full eternity rings are not as common, partly because they cost a lot more but also they have to be made to order as once the stones are set the ring size cannot be easily altered.

The love knot is a very popular design for brooches. They consist of two rope-like pieces that are twisted together to form a bow and they represent the joining together of two people. Love knots can be made from various metals.

Serpent or snake jewellery symbolizes wisdom and when found with its tail in its mouth it symbolizes eternal love.

Lizards and frogs can be symbolic of wedded bliss.

Musical instruments featured in jewellery can have symbolic meanings. For example, the harp or lyre symbolizes love and the trumpet usually heralds an announcement of good news such as an engagement.

The secret language of flowers was very popular with the Victorians and Edwardians and they took great delight in the hidden meanings it could convey. The jewellery of this period often adopts these floral themes. For example:

Ivy stands for fidelity in marriage or, when wrapped around a crucifix, religious faith.

Forget-me-knots represent true love, especially when circumstances have forced lovers apart.

Ferns are associated with sincerity.

Pansies convey thoughtfulness.

Gemstones can be used to spell out a hidden word, for example, a ring might have Rubies, Emeralds, Garnets, Amethysts, Rubies and Diamonds. These spell out the word 'REGARD'. These items were usually made with imitation stones rather than the real thing.

Mizpah brooches

Mizpah brooches have a religious significance. The Hebrew word 'mizpah', meaning 'watchtower', is used as a greeting to say 'Lord watch between me and thee'. The brooches typically feature two hearts; one heart has some bible text engraved with 'mizpah' over it and the other has three symbols: a cross, an anchor and a heart to represent faith, hope and charity.

Mourning jewellery

Queen Victoria promoted the fashion for mourning jewellery after she was widowed in 1861. In keeping with the custom of the times, she dressed only in black and, not wishing to forgo wearing jewellery altogether, she selected pieces made of Whitby jet as a suitably sombre expression of her grief. Few people observe such strict mourning rituals today but jet remains an attractive natural material. If you felt like reviving the tradition you could probably find an attractive Victorian jet brooch for less than £50.

9

Medals, coins and stamps

Many British households have a military medal or two tucked away in a drawer, the proud reminder of a relative who saw action in the First or Second World War, or maybe a campaign even further back in time, like the Boer War or the Crimean War. Unless you come from a service background or have studied military history you probably won't know much about these medals. Most people have heard of the Victoria Cross and the George Cross but do you know when they were first introduced, what they were for and how many have been awarded altogether? And what do you think they would be worth today?

Many more of us hang on to old coins and stamps – inherited from a collector in the family, perhaps, or the result of a childhood hobby – in the belief that they may be valuable. They are money, after all. But how much are they really worth? This chapter will help you to find out.

Medals

Elizabeth I was the first English monarch to have campaign medals struck and these were awarded to the commanders responsible for the defeat of the Spanish Armada in 1588. The ordinary men were not honoured.

There has always been a distinction drawn between the officers and other ranks and it is one that persisted until 1993, when the whole system of awarding different medals for merit was reformed.

There are two categories of British war medal: the campaign medal and the gallantry medal. The difference is that campaign medals are commemorative and are issued to everyone who has taken part in a battle and gallantry medals are given only to those individuals (including non-military personnel) who have been singled out for their bravery.

Campaign medals

These medals commemorate specific military campaigns. They sometimes have additional bars to signify an important battle within that campaign.

Trafalgar: 1805 These medals were made by Matthew Boulton from Birmingham at his own expense and were issued to the survivors of the Battle of Trafalgar. Around the edge the medal is inscribed 'From Boulton to the Heroes of Trafalgar'. On one side there is a portrait of Nelson and on the other a coat of arms. They were made from gold, silver, bronze gilt, bronze and pewter and were awarded according to rank. Present-day values reflect this and range from about £200 for a pewter medal to around £7000 for a gold one.

Naval General Service Medal: 1793–1840 This medal was issued to all personnel who served in the Navy during the Napoleonic Wars (1793–1815), the Battle of Algiers (1816), Navarino (1827) and Syria (1840). There were 24,000 of these medals issued altogether, with an astounding range of 231 different bars representing a multitude of battles. It is the rarity of the bar that determines the value, with '8th April 1814' fetching around £2000 down to the most common examples, which include 'Syria', 'Egypt' and 'Lissa' at around £150 each.

Military General Service: 1793–1814 This medal was awarded to Wellington's troops for their victories in Spain and Portugal. It depicts the Iron Duke kneeling before Queen Victoria as she crowns him with a laurel wreath of victory. Issued in 1847, there were 25,650 in total, with 25 bars. The rarest is the 'Benevente' bar, worth around £2000, and the most common is 'St Sebastian', which is valued at around £200.

The Waterloo Medal: 1815 (British and Allied) This was the first medal produced by the government and each one has the recipient's name engraved on the edges. This is a godsend to medal collectors as it allows them to check the name in the service records. Although it is known as the Waterloo medal, and was awarded to those who took part in that battle on 18 June 1815, it was also given to those who saw action at Ligny and Quatre Bras on 16 June. There are very few of these medals surviving in good condition, largely because they were issued just a year after the conflict and so they were often worn rather than put away. Prices range from £200 to £400, with those medals issued to the regiments that suffered high casualties being the most valuable, while those issued to regiments with relatively low casualties, or those that saw no action at all, such as General Colville's Reserve Division, are worth less.

Crimea Medal: 1854–56 Many campaign medals were issued following the Battle of Waterloo. The Crimea Medal was the only one to be awarded for services against a major power, in this case Russia after it had invaded Turkey. Medals awarded to those who participated in the charges, both light and heavy, are the most collectable. There are five bars associated with this medal: 'Alma', 'Inkerman', 'Azoff', 'Balaklava' and 'Sebastopol'. Values range from £45 to £200.

The Queen's South Africa Medal: 1899–1902 These medals were awarded for services during the second Boer War. A large number were issued and included, for the first time, personnel serving in divisions such as the balloon and photographic, cyclists, field canteens, and so on. A few were also issued to native Africans. There are 26 additional bars associated with this medal, covering, for example, the Defence of Ladysmith and the Relief of Kimberley,

but the most famous relates to the Siege of Mafeking. This is where around 1500 men under the command of Baden-Powell held a fort for 215 days against the Boers, who numbered many thousands, until reinforcements arrived. Prices vary from as much as £850 for Mafeking, down to £50 for Cape Colony.

First World War (1914–18)

The three most common campaign medals associated with the First World War were affectionately dubbed 'Pip, Squeak and Wilfred' after the names of a trio of popular comic strip characters of the time.

The 1914 and 1914–15 Stars (Pip)

These stars were the first of several issued for service during the First World War. It is a bronze star-shaped medal with two crossed swords on the front circled by a laurel wreath surmounted by a crown. There are then three variations: The first was issued to those who served in France and Belgium between 5 August and 22 November 1914. (This version has the date 1914 across the front.) The second was issued to those who had actually been under fire and is known as the 'Mons Star'. (This version has the addition of a bar with the dates 5th Aug and 22nd Nov 1914.) The third star is known as the 1914–15 star and was issued to those who saw service between 5 August 1914 and 31 December 1915. (This version has the dates 1914–15 across the front.) These medals were made from bronze and range in value from £10 to £40, depending on the regiment. The rear of these medals are all inscribed with the name and regiment of the recipient.

The British War Medal 1914–20 (Squeak)

This medal was made to commemorate some of the most terrible battles of the First World War. The front of the medal bears the profile of King George V and the rear St George on horseback, slaying a dragon. The recipient's details are found around the edge. Between 1914 and 1920 6.5 million in silver were issued and 110,000 were issued in bronze to native labour corps. As the bronze medals were produced in comparatively small numbers, their value is greater than their silver counterparts: £15 for silver, £30 for bronze.

The Victory Medal 1914–18 (Wilfred)

This medal was issued to all personnel who had previously received one of the stars and the British War Medal. It is quite common therefore to find these three medals together, referred to as a 'trio'. This medal bears the picture of 'Victory' on the front and the wording 'the great war for civilisation' on the back. As with the British War Medal, the recipient's details are found around the edge. There were no bars issued with these medals, due to their large numbers. The only exception is the Oak Leaf, which can be found on some of the Victory medals, namely those personnel mentioned in despatches. A trio is worth about £50 but a Victory medal on its own will be a lot less.

The death plaque Although not strictly known as a medal, this large 'coin' bearing the profile of Britannia with the deceased's name was issued to the families of those killed in action. This plaque, along with a trio set, is worth somewhere in the region of £100. Death plaques issued to a female killed in action are more valuable.

Second World War (1939–45)
The Second World War Campaign Stars

1939–45 There are eight variations of this medal, which is made from a copper and zinc alloy. They are all similar, all being a six-pointed star with a crown cipher of King George VI in the centre. The cipher is surrounded by the dates or name of the appropriate campaign as follows:

1939/45 (Battle of Britain)
The Atlantic Star
The Air Crew Europe
The Africa Star
The Pacific Star
The Burma Star
The Italy Star
The France and Germany Star

Most of them were not personalized with any details of the recipient. They were issued with a variety of ribbons, all of which are symbolic, for example, a blue, yellow and black striped ribbon was issued with the Air Crew Europe Star. The blue represents the sky, the yellow the searchlights and the black for night flights. Their values range from £3 to £50. The Battle of Britain star, if issued with a name on the reverse, and the Air Crew Europe are the most valuable.

The Defence Medal: 3 September 1939 – 2 September 1945 This is the most common Second World War medal as it was issued to members of the Home Guard and Civil Defence. The medal bears a royal coat of arms and the wording 'Defence Medal'. They are issued with a green, orange and black ribbon, which symbolizes the British Isles (green), the bombing fires (orange) and the blackouts (black). Because so many were issued they are only worth a few pounds.

The War Medal: 3 September 1939 – 2 September 1945 This medal was awarded to all full-time personnel of the armed forces, whether operational or not. It features a lion and the dates. They were mostly made from cupro-nickel, plus a very small number of silver ones. Their value ranges from £3 to £15.

Gallantry medals

Gallantry medals were issued to both military and civilian personnel to acknowledge acts of bravery or gallantry during wartime. The most important are: the Victoria Cross, the George Cross, the DSO, the DFC and the DFM.

The Victoria Cross (VC) was created as a result of the carnage of the Crimean War (1854–6) even though hostilities had ceased a good twelve months before the first award was made. The Queen herself took a great interest in the design and in fact suggested bronze as a suitable material. It was decided at the outset that the VC would break with established tradition and be awarded simply 'For Valour', the military rank of the recipient having no bearing on the matter. Inspired by the Queen's suggestion, it was thought fitting to take the bronze from Russian guns captured in the Crimea. But it seems that the engineer who examined the two chosen 18-pounders in Woolwich Barracks failed to notice that the guns were clearly of Chinese, not Russian, origin!

The VC is awarded for exceptional gallantry and as such is the most prized award a subject of the realm can receive. Since Queen Victoria presented the first one a total of 1354 have been issued so far. (Eight of them have been forfeited for misconduct.) Of these, 832 were awarded to the Army, 107 to the Navy, 31 to the RAF and the remainder to Commonwealth units. One was awarded to 'The US Unknown Soldier, Arlington Cemetery'. The youngest recipient of a Victoria Cross was just 15 and the oldest was 69. Since the end of the Second World War the VC has only been awarded 11 times, the most recent being two during the Falklands War in 1982.

Since the VC is awarded for acts of bravery 'in the face of the enemy', there are those that believe that the changing nature of warfare, with less close contact between opposing forces, may result in no more VCs being awarded in the future.

There are many factors to take into account when valuing a VC but on the rare occasions that they turn up for public auction they fetch many thousands of pounds.

The George Cross (GC) was introduced in 1940, during the height of the bombing of British cities by the Luftwaffe. The GC can be awarded to both military and civilian personnel for acts of great heroism performed in any circumstances other than battle. There have been 399 awarded to date, a few of these being translated from other medals; 155 have been awarded to civilians and four have gone to women including the wartime SOE agents Violette Szabo and Odette Sansom. One was also awarded collectively to the island of Malta in 1942 for the population's heroic resistance to enemy bombing raids. Their values at auction range from £3000 to £6000.

The Distinguished Service Order: 1886

(DSO) ranks below the VC. It was originally restricted to officers above the rank of captain but following the 1993 review it is now open to all ranks. It is no longer awarded for gallantry, this now being in the remit of the Conspicuous Gallantry Cross. Originally the medal was made from gold and enamel but from 1889 it was made in silver gilt. Value depends on rarity. The original gold medals are very rare, as are those issued during the reign of Edward VII as no major wars took place during his reign. The gold medals are worth in excess of £1500 and the silver ones would be around £300.

The Distinguished Flying Cross: 1918

(DFC) dates from 1918, when the Royal Flying Corps became the Royal Air Force. It is awarded for gallantry in action whilst engaged in flying operations. Just over 1000 were awarded in the First World War and nearly 21,000 in the Second World War. Values, which can range from £300 to £600, are dependent on the specific reason for issue, the Battle of Britain being a particularly important one.

The Distinguished Flying Medal (DFM)

was instituted in June 1918 at the same time as the DFC and other RAF awards for acts of valour by aircrew, NCOs and men whilst flying in active operations against the enemy. Fewer than 200 were awarded up until 1939 but about 6700 were awarded between then and the end of the war in 1945. The DFM was abolished in 1993, when the honours system was reformed and the DFC was opened to all ranks. The value range is similar to that of the DFC.

The Military Medal: 1916

was given to other ranks for acts of bravery in the field. Over 120,000 were issued during the First World War and 1600 during the Second World War, making this medal one of the most common gallantry awards. Value is dependent on the date of issue and can range from £45 to £400.

The Conspicuous Gallantry Cross

came in after the 1993 review and it replaces the DSO (when awarded for gallantry), the DCM, CGM (Navy) and CGM (RAF). The Distinguished Service Medal (DSM), Military Medal (MM), Distinguished Flying Medal (DFM) and Air Force Medal (AFM) have all been discontinued. There is as yet no serious market for these awards although the rarity value of those that it replaces will certainly increase over time.

Non-military medals

Medals are not just awarded for military service, of course. People can get them in almost any sphere of life, including politics, education or sport. For example, medals were struck to commemorate Pitt's role in the repeal of the Stamp Act in 1766 and others celebrate the arrival of carrier pigeons in Paris during the siege of 1871.

As far as value is concerned, anything made of gold, such as Masonic medals or Olympic medals, will at least have a bullion value. The most attractive to collectors are those that have a clear provenance traceable to someone famous. If you have an interesting medal, try typing the words of the inscription into a search engine on the internet and see what comes up. You never know, you might just strike gold.

Coins

The use of coins goes back to Asia Minor in the seventh century BC and the
ancient Greeks and Romans both developed a very sophisticated system of currency,
using different metals – gold, silver, bronze or copper.

The first truly British (as opposed to Roman)
coin was the silver penny, which was issued
in about AD790 by King Offa of Mercia. They
were able to cast 240 coins from one pound
of sterling silver and so the British system
of currency was invented: 240 pence to
the pound.

When it comes to valuing British coins today,
the gold sovereign and the silver crown are
the collector's favourites. Both have a bullion
value to back them up, although this is of
real significance only for the gold coins, and
prices in the trade will fluctuate to reflect any
changes in this value. For sovereigns, crowns
and all other collectable coins their value
depends on just two factors: date and
condition.

Sovereigns and crowns
Assuming a coin is not a forgery (and there
are quite a few of those in circulation), establishing how old it is is simple because the
year is marked on every piece that has come
out of the Royal Mint. But value will depend
more on rarity than age so the first thing to
do when you are assessing a coin is to check
the reference books to find out what year
it was. For example, a 1925 sovereign will
be worth between £50 and £95, depending
on its condition, whereas one minted the
following year would be valued at £500–2500.
The value of a crown minted in 1933

(£10–£250) shows a similar disparity compared to one issued in 1934 (£300–£900).

Condition, condition, condition
People often fall into the trap of overestimating
the condition of their coins and are consequently disappointed with the prices that
dealers offer. But it is probably true to say
that coins represent the only area of the
antiques trade where near perfection is pretty
much an essential. Professionals and serious
collectors (numismatists) have developed a
sophisticated scale to describe the various
states that a coin can end up in.

Bits and pieces
Twentieth-century coins in circulation in Britain
before decimalization in 1971 were: the half
crown, the florin, the shilling, the sixpenny bit,
the threepenny bit, the penny, the halfpenny
and the farthing. These are not really worth
collecting, with one or two notable exceptions:
the 1933 penny, for example, is now worth
thousands of pounds because so few of
them were struck.

Until 1944 the threepenny bit was a silver
coin and traditionalists will know that these
were the little gifts that once ended up in the
Christmas pudding every year. You would be
lucky to get even £1 for one today unless it
was a rare year, say 1893, when it might be
worth about £120. The replacement 12-edged

This set of coins minted in Queen Victoria's Golden Jubilee year, 1887, is now worth about £5000

threepenny bits issued during the Second World War were made of nickel and brass and have no value today.

Proof sets

Proof sets were introduced in 1826 and were often given to foreign diplomats. They were intended for investment rather than circulation and sets were invariably sold for higher than the circulation value of the coins, thus becoming investment or collectors' items from day one. It is important to have their original presentation boxes or cases, together with any literature that came with them. Proof sets usually consist of a full set of coins in current circulation although some-times non-current proof coins will be included. They are always collectable, with the value depending as usual on age, rarity and con-dition. An 1853 set of 16 coins ranging from a quarter farthing to a sovereign might fetch £20,000 while sets from the 1980s could be worth anything from £10 to £1000.

You may have come across proof sets that various manufacturers have produced, often in limited edition. It is too soon to tell whether these will appreciate in value but for the moment I would advise you to stick to sets issued by the Royal Mint.

Maundy money

Every year, on Maundy Thursday, the day before Good Friday, the Queen gives a boxed set of small silver coins to each one of a small group of people equal to the monarch's age, in a ceremony held in various cathedrals around the country. The coins are minted especially for the occasion, and come in four denominations – 1p, 2p, 3p and 4p – so in total they have a face value of 10p. This custom of giving alms at Easter dates back to 1662 and the reign of Charles II. Today's recipients are not exactly the deserving poor as they were in the past but are an equal number of Christian men and women over the age of 65 who have been nominated for their service to the community. A set from 1763 is now worth around £120 and a set from 1922 around £50.

Quality scale for coins

Coin experts and serious collectors (numismatists) use the following scale to describe the quality of coins, ranging from the most worn to the most pristine. The quality of a coin does not in itself determine its value, however. Rarity is just as important a consideration.

Poor
Inscriptions worn off, the date illegible and only the faintest outline of the design visible. Coins in this condition will only have a resale value if exceptionally rare.

Fair
Considerable wear over the whole coin, and high spots worn through. Coins of this grade are only collectable if extremely rare. Collectors' books do not quote values for coins in this condition.

Fine (F)
Worn over whole area, but with only the highest spots worn completely through. This is the lowest standard at which dealers will normally be prepared to quote a value.

Very Fine (VF)
Detail clear, evidence of very limited circulation. Detail remains on high spots. Traces of mint lustre may linger amongst the letters of the inscription.

Extremely Fine (EF)
Very slight wear on high spots. All other detail clear and sharp. Much mint lustre may remain. Will probably appear 'uncirculated' to the untrained eye.

Uncirculated (Unc)
No wear at all, although it is possible for the design not to be fully struck up in the minting process and there may be abrasions. Older coins may be tarnished or toned.

Collectors' guides also feature two even higher grades:

Brilliant Uncirculated (BU)
Usually implies full mint lustre.

FDC (Fleur de Coin)
Perfect mint state, with no abrasions or marks, and full lustre. Usually refers to proof coins or coins from sealed mint sets. A proof coin is one that has been struck using specially prepared dies and blanks. It may also have been put through the minting process twice, with extra pressure to ensure the die is filled. The fields on proof coins are normally highly polished and they usually have very sharp edges.

Stamps

It was the British who invented the postage stamp and the first ones – the famous penny black and the twopenny blue – went on sale in May 1840. Other countries quickly cottoned on to the idea and it was not long before every nation in the world saw the advantages of raising revenue by issuing stamps.

There are two main types of stamp collection: the 'schoolboy' collection and the 'serious' collection. Most fall into the 'schoolboy' category and you would be lucky to find anything of value here, though you should always check just in case you have something out of the ordinary. Even if you are only collecting as a hobby, always make sure that you mount your stamps carefully with proper stamp hinges in a loose-leaf album.

For the true philatelist, value is a question of condition, rarity and theme. The best way to learn about these is to consult a specialist dealer or to work your way through one of the comprehensive price guides. Stamps are unusual in the world of collectables because you may find that the 'perfect condition' rule that is paramount in other fields could well give way to the trump card of 'rarity' here. Printers can make mistakes and the post office authorities are not always as eagle-eyed as they should be; printing errors, such as an upside-down image or a missing value, and 'imperforates' (sheets without perforations), are always swiftly rectified but will produce the few rare examples that are guaranteed to get any collector's blood racing. A unique Swedish 1855 three skilling yellow (which should have been green) was sold for £900,000 in 1996.

The penny black

The penny black, a small black stamp with the profile of Queen Victoria on it, is well worth seeking out even though millions of them were issued in 1840–41. You could expect to get up to £3000 for an unused stamp in perfect condition and even a used one might bring in around £150.

The penny black was discontinued after a year and replaced with the penny red for two reasons: firstly because the black ink cross initially used as a mark to cancel the stamp to indicate that it had been through the post did not show up and secondly because the subsequent remedy for this, a red ink postmark, was all too easily washed off and people realized they could cheat the system and re-use old stamps.

The twopenny blue

The twopenny blue was issued at the same time as the penny black and it remained in circulation until 1880. During that time it went through three important changes in design. Twopenny blues of the original design are extremely rare and are now worth £180 (unperforated). Like the penny blacks, the twopenny blues were printed in sheets of 240 that had to be cut up with scissors as the stamps were not perforated.

A sheet of six twopenny blues in mint condition

The penny red

The penny red replaced the penny black in 1841 and the same design remained in use for nearly 40 years. Penny reds were the first stamps to be perforated and printed on sheets with a serial number (corresponding to the particular batch printed from a single plate). An unused penny red in perfect condition with a rare plate number could fetch in excess of £1000 while a used one in fair condition might be worth around £150–200.

First-day covers

First-day covers are aimed purely at collectors. They usually consist of a full set of stamps, generally four or five, incorporated onto an envelope. The idea is that collectors mail these envelopes to themselves so that they arrive with a postmark dated for the first day of issue.

10

Toys

Old toys in the cupboard: instant nostalgia. They have the power to turn us back into little boys and girls again in an instant. But the problem with toys, when it comes to assessing their value as collectables, is that children play with them, they get dirty, broken, bits go missing, their carefully designed packaging all thrown out with the Christmas wrapping paper.

For the serious collector, the best toys, like the best books, are those that have never been touched by human hand. Failing this, they have to be very old or very rare, preferably both at the same time. If you have any toys stored away unloved in the attic, how do you know if they are worth selling? Or should they be heading for the dustbin? The most popular areas for collecting are: dolls, teddy bears, board games and vehicles.

Dolls

Since the fifteenth century, when the first European dolls were produced, makers have tried all sorts of materials in their quest to find a flexible medium that would allow them to produce a toy that not only looked appealing to a child but would also stand up to a fair amount of rough handling.

Materials

The first dolls to be made commercially came from Germany and they were made of wood, hand-carved, and dressed in the style of German women of the period. The heads were of a simple construction and the facial features were painted on.

Mass-production of a sort began in the early eighteenth century, when the makers started using moulds, which meant that a doll's fingers, toes and facial features could be represented more naturalistically. Wax was the first material that the makers turned to for their moulded dolls. Solid wax dolls of this period were very expensive to buy at the time and are still highly regarded – they keep their value because there are not many left. Germany again led the field when they started to adapt *papier mâché* for dolls' heads in around 1810. The wax often peels away in parts, revealing the paper beneath.

Ball joints were developed around 1850 and gave the dolls some flexibility. Imperfections were covered with gesso, a mixture of plaster of Paris and glue, before the dolls were painted. Bisque-headed dolls first appeared around the same time and German and French makers were able to capitalize on the popularity of this type for the next hundred years. Early examples have a leather body stuffed with sawdust or cork. Bisque is a type of fine porcelain and the technique gets its name from the fact that the china acquires a 'biscuity' texture – it is not glazed, so it has quite a dull appearance and feels slightly rough to the touch. Bisque porcelain allows great definition and so these dolls were made with a variety of lifelike expressions. Some have glass eyes and realistic-looking teeth.

Celluloid was first developed in 1869. It was initially considered an ideal material for dolls because, like bisque, it could be moulded to produce fine details but with the added advantage that it was more durable. The drawbacks were quickly discovered, however, the main one being that celluloid is highly flammable, which makes it an unsuitable material for a child's toy. The other problem is that it cracks and dents quite easily. Celluloid dolls have yet to secure a place as worthwhile collectables.

The modern doll-making industry was revolutionized in the 1950s, when hard plastic was first introduced, swiftly followed by vinyl, the most common material in use today.

The trade divides dolls into three main categories: fashion dolls, *bébé* dolls and character dolls.

Fashion dolls originated in France in the middle of the nineteenth century. They were modelled as miniature adults, with a defined female shape, wearing clothing in the fashion of the day. They were often used as mannequins in the salons of high-quality couturiers to show off to their customers the clothes that were available that season.

Bébé **dolls** are also traditionally French, dating from the same period as fashion dolls. Pierre François Jumeau made the first *bébé* doll in 1855. It was modelled on a female baby, with chubby limbs and a rounded stomach. From around 1870, German manufacturers began making large numbers of *bébé* dolls. They had real hair, or mohair, and glass eyes, and a feature that has delighted little girls ever since – eyelids that open and shut when the doll is rocked back and forth.

Character dolls are a nineteenth-century German invention. They were often modelled on real people, sometimes in a special pose, and have very lifelike features. Dolls with non-European, especially Oriental, features were particularly popular though they were not as cute as the cupid dolls or 'kewpies'. These are indeed 'cupid-like', with round bodies, very large eyes, a smiling expression and a tuft or topknot of hair. They were inspired by the American children's illustrator Rosie O'Neill and were made by Kestner & Co of Germany.

Valuing a doll

To the serious collector, the most important feature of a doll is the head. In most cases the name of the manufacturer can be found on the back of the head, just under the hairline, and next to this there should be a reference number. Cracks, chips, overpainting and missing eyes all detract from the value. Watch out for touched-up eyebrows, a

Bébé **doll dating from the late nineteenth century**

common area of overpainting. Original eyebrows are usually feather-like so if you see a solid black line someone has almost certainly done a bit of clumsy DIY restoration. The condition of a doll's clothing and hair is less important.

The best fashion dolls you are likely to come across are those made by François Gaultier and Bru Jeune in France in the second half of the nineteenth century. These are currently worth a good £2000 or more. Germany dominates the *bébé* doll market, with some of the best examples coming from Simon & Halbig and Kammer & Reinhardt, though the French doll-maker Pierre François Jumeau remains the master. One of his *bébé* dolls, dating from 1855 to 1900, could be worth £4000 or more. Kestner's kewpie dolls, made between 1880 and 1920, were so popular that they are not especially rare and so you might be able to pick one up today for £100 or so. As ever, rarity is the name of the game, so it is important to do your research into the different doll-makers and the system of reference numbers they used.

The Barbie phenomenon

A doll does not have to be an antique to be worth a lot of money. If you have one of the first Barbie dolls, boxed and perfect, you could be looking at £2000 or more. Throw in all the accessories that went with her and you can add another £500 or so. Barbie is the most successful doll ever made. She first came out of the factory of the American firm Mattel in 1959 and has never stopped. The earliest Barbie dolls were mounted on a stand and so they have holes in their feet.

The Pedigree company introduced Barbie's British counterpart, Sindy, in 1962. Like Barbie, Sindy was typically blonde-haired and blue-eyed. Pedigree also produced a range of dark-skinned dolls and these are very collectable today.

Teddy bears

The teddy bear was invented in 1902 by Margaret Steiff, a toy manufacturer based in Germany.

She was inspired by the story of the American President, Theodore ('Teddy') Roosevelt, who apparently refused to shoot a bear cub that was tethered to a tree as he felt it would have been unsporting. When Steiff made her first toy bear cub she called it 'Teddy's Bear' after the caption that was given to the photograph in the newspapers and the name caught on.

Steiff Bears (1903 to date)

Steiff's teddy bears were popular right from the start, though they were always expensive compared to other stuffed toys. They are now regarded as the best in the world. Made from mohair and stuffed with straw, the Steiff bear typically has a long snout, very long front arms with large paws, and a humped back. They were made in various colours, the most common being golden. The rarest are the black bears, which sold less well, and the cinnamon-coloured ones, which often had their lives cut short because the dye used to make the mohair rot. If you find a bear in good condition with a button marked 'Steiff' stitched to one of its ears, hold your breath – it could be worth thousands.

Chad Valley (*c.*1897–1978)

Chad Valley was a Birmingham-based British toy manufacturing company that started producing teddy bears in 1920. They are easily identified by the Chad Valley label stitched to one of the feet. If the label is missing, look out for an animal made out of orange mohair, with a fat body, short limbs, amber and black glass eyes and a heavily stitched nose. Chad Valley bears were stuffed with kapok, a lightweight natural fibre that gives a much softer feel to the toy than straw.

Merrythought Limited (est. 1930)
Merrythought were a Shropshire-based teddy bear manufacturing company. Their bears are similar in appearance to the Chad Valley bears but have a celluloid button in the ear as well as a fabric foot label.

J. K. Farnell & Co (1897–1968)
Farnell's was a famous London-based toy manufacturer. Their bears look similar to the Steiff bears. It is believed that the children's author A. A. Milne bought a Farnell bear for his son, Christopher Robin, and this gave him the idea for his Winnie the Pooh stories (though it is believed he borrowed Pooh's name from a Canadian bear in London Zoo at the time). Like the Chad Valley and Merrythought bears, a decent Farnell teddy could be worth up to £600 or more.

A Steiff teddy bear

Vehicles

Every kind of vehicle imaginable has been reproduced in toy form at some time or other. Trains have always been top of the enthusiast's list, followed by cars.

Trains
Working model train sets were produced in Britain by Frank Hornby of Liverpool from around 1920, although they had been made abroad as far back as 1850. Hornby challenged the German domination of toy manufacture by developing his own range of trains with the slogan 'British Toys for British Boys'.

Engines could be clockwork, steam or, from 1925, electric. From 1930 Hornby made realistic and accurate copies of real trains. He also produced all the accessories needed to create a railway. The smallest range made from 1938 was called 'Dublo', taking its name from the width of the track, being 00 (double '0') gauge. The electrically powered engines quickly became Hornby's most successful range, easily outselling the cheaper clockwork sets being sold at the same time. So the rarity principle applies again: clockwork engines are more collectable than the electric ones. You could be looking at as much as £1000 for a good clockwork engine made in the 1900s. And the engine is the most desirable part of any train set, though collectors are always on the lookout for a tender with advertising panels. Original boxes in good condition plus accessories all contribute to the value.

In spite of Hornby, some German train sets are still desirable. Look for Marklin (est. 1859), Bing (1863–1933) and Carette & Cie (est. 1886 by the Frenchman George Carette). Hornby itself was taken over in 1964 by Triang and the name changed to Triang Hornby. It changed again in 1971, to Hornby Railways.

Cars

Frank Hornby created the first Dinky toy cars in 1934 because he wanted some accessories for his train sets. He produced replicas of a wide range of vehicles. They were originally sold in sets of eight and were quite expensive. Complete boxed sets from this period are now worth about £1000. In 1947 he went in for larger commercial vehicles, mainly lorries. These 'super toys' as he called them had advertising logos; the Weetabix lorry is the one to look for – it's extremely rare.

A Hornby train set

Unfortunately, when Hornby was taken over by Triang in 1964, the quality of their toys fell with perhaps the exception of spacecraft made to accompany the *Thunderbirds* television series. In 1979 the Dinky factory closed.

The most collectable Hornby Dinkies are those made before the Triang takeover. Cars in their original boxes, especially unopened, are the most valuable.

Hornby's main rival from the middle of the twentieth century onwards was a firm called Mettoy, which launched the 'Corgi' range of toy vehicles in 1956. They introduced various improvements, such as doors that opened, plastic windows and spring suspension. Corgi made the most successful toy car ever – a model of the Aston Martin DB5 used in the James Bond film *Goldfinger*. They sold over three million of these but who knows how many remain in perfect-boxed condition. If you do find one that has never been near a small boy it will net you around £100 but the price will quickly drop to around £25 if its original box is missing.

Another important rival toy manufacturer was a firm called Lesney, which launched the very successful 'Matchbox' range. These were affordable pocket-sized toys that were sold in a box the same size and shape as a matchbox. Their most famous range was 'models of yesteryear', which were aimed at adult collectors. For this reason it is not uncommon to find them in very good condition.

Board games

It is believed board games have been in existence since Roman times. Roman soldiers based at Hadrian's Wall are known to have played a number of games, including dice and ball games, for the purpose of gambling.

Chess

The earliest known board game is chess, the earliest version of which dates back to sixth-century India, when it was called 'shaturanga' where two players acted as rajas (or kings) and fought battles between four armies, which were divided up into infantry, cavalry, elephants and boatmen. Chess as we know it today appeared in Europe at the end of the fifteenth century. The first international chess tournament was held in London in 1851, by which time the basic rules of the game had been published. They would have used chess pieces based on a new design by Howard Staunton that he patented in 1847.

Most chess pieces made from ivory, with half of the set being stained red, were made in Burma. Complete sets are quite valuable, maybe £200 or more for one made in 1900. Wooden pieces are worth less than ivory ones.

Monopoly

By the 1870s the development of inexpensive wood-pulp paper combined with cheap methods of printing led to the invention and mass-production of a variety of affordable board games. The Victorians loved them.

The most popular board game of all time is Monopoly, which was dreamed up by the Parker Brothers of Salem, Massachusetts, in 1935. Waddingtons acquired the rights to produce the British version of the game and it is alleged that the company contributed to the war effort by concealing printed maps inside the sets that were distributed to the troops behind enemy lines.

Millions of Monopoly sets have been sold worldwide and only sets produced in the first year and in pristine condition will be worth anything. If you find the words 'Patent Applied for 1935' printed on the middle of the board you could be looking at £100 or so, but if it says 'Patent Approved' forget it.

Escalado

This is a popular horseracing game made by Chad Valley. It involves lead horses being pushed along by a vibrating sheet that is operated by a crank handle. Four horses make their way down the 'field'. Bets would be placed by individuals, the winner collecting the prize money. It was apparently a favourite game of the late Queen Mother. A complete working set from the 1920s would be worth £25–50.

11

Miscellaneous

Books, cigarette cards, postcards and autographs are highly collectable; indeed, their very nature seems to invite collection, in a bookcase or in an album. Furthermore, many of these paper-based items exert an emotional hold that can be transferred from one owner to the next. Lots of people would be willing to pay good money for an early edition of their favourite novel, for example, or the signed photograph of a movie idol.

This chapter will help to give you some idea of the kinds of books, cards and autographs that are likely to attract collectors. It will also look at a miscellany of other sought-after items people often keep tucked away, including lace, linens and samplers, and what I've called 'old technology' – those mechanical objects such as musical boxes, gramophones and still cameras which, despite being superseded by more modern equivalents, still have the capacity to fascinate us.

Books

The serious book collector is usually only interested in first editions, and not only that – these first editions should be in immaculate condition (no dog-ears, no foxing, no worm-holes) and come with an untorn, unstained, unfaded original dust jacket. Quite a tall order, considering that deterioration tends to start as soon as you open a book and given that paper responds quite badly to sunlight, heat, damp, dust, dry air, insects and sticky fingers. A true bibliophile does not want a book to be marked in any way at all unless the notes in the margins and the signature or dedication are in the author's own hand, in which case the value will shoot up considerably.

Establishing whether a book is a first edition is fairly straightforward: towards the front of the book, on what is known as the copyright page, you should find the words 'first published' followed by the year. There are exceptions to this general rule, especially with books published more than a hundred years ago, but a dealer will always put you straight.

You should bear in mind that not all first editions are worth a fortune, though: it all depends on supply and demand. There are some books that nobody wants and others that everyone is dying to get their hands on. The joy of collecting books is that they don't have to be all that old to be valuable and their authors don't have to be dead to put money in your pocket.

Two very popular areas for collectors are exploration and discovery and children's books. Within these fields the quality of the book's binding and the nature of the illustrations will have a strong influence on value.

Exploration and discovery

Captain James Cook's accounts of his voyages, such as *Making Discoveries in the Southern Hemisphere* (1773), are quite rare, and the published journals of James Bruce and Mungo Park, who both explored Africa in the late eighteenth century, are also sought after. David Livingstone's *Missionary Travels and Researches in South Africa* (1857) has pull-out maps and a steel-engraved portrait of the author and became a bestseller in Britain.

Children's books

Early books for children, such as John Bunyan's *A Book for Boys and Girls* (1686) had a lofty moral tone. Three volumes of fairy stories compiled by the German brothers Grimm appeared in English translation in 1823 and Hans Christian Andersen's famous stories for children were translated from the Danish in the 1840s. Lewis Carroll's *Alice's Adventures in Wonderland* (1865) and *Through the Looking Glass* (1871), which contain John Tenniel's marvellous illustrations, are also worth looking out for.

Among more recent works, first editions of A. A. Milne's collections of children's verse, *When We Were Very Young* (1924) and *Now We Are Six* (1927), are worth around £8,000 in good condition. And a first-edition copy of Beatrix Potter's *The Tale of Peter Rabbit*, published privately in 1901, could fetch as much as £50,000. Even first editions of J. K. Rowling's *Harry Potter and the Philosopher's Stone*, which was published in a print run of just 500 copies in hardback in 1997, are now reputed to be worth around £25,000!

Cigarette cards, postcards and autographs

Cigarette cards

Cigarette cards first appeared in 1870 and the tobacco companies went on issuing them until the end of the Second World War. There are now well over 5000 different sets available to the collector, in packs of 50, 25 or 20 cards linked by theme.

In the nineteenth century cigarettes used to be sold in thin paper packs stiffened with a piece of card (a 'stiffie'). Sometime in the 1880s W. D. & H. O. Wills of Bristol started to put printed cards in their cigarette packs. These had a picture on one side and text on the back. The very first set to be issued featured the kings and queens of England and other subjects quickly followed, including sporting personalities, film stars, transport, technology, and animals, birds and flowers. Before long all the major tobacco companies had jumped on the cigarette card bandwagon.

Smokers (and children) soon started to collect these cards and to swap them so that they ended up with a full set. Unfortunately, many people decided to gum their backs and stick them directly onto the pages of an album. This is disastrous and these cards are worthless today because you can't see the descriptions on the backs of them and it would spoil them to remove them. The good news is that other collectors bought albums that allowed them to slip the cards into slots or mounts on the page and these can be taken out without doing any damage.

Serious collectors of cigarette cards are generally only interested in complete sets, and factors such as condition and subject matter are also crucial. Rarity is important, too, and a collector will be looking not just for unusual subjects but also for those sets that came with the less common brands of cigarette, especially from tobacco companies that were not in business for very long. Cards produced by Taddy, Cope Brothers or Black Cat are rare and are therefore more collectable – this is why a set of 20 made by Taddy with a circus theme would be worth about £2500 while a run-of-the-mill set of 50 butterflies from W. D. & H. O. Wills would only fetch a fraction of that. Value also increases if there is some sort of crossover; people in the market for sporting memorabilia may be interested in cigarette cards relating to their own particular interest. A set of 50 cards issued by Cope Brothers with a golfing theme, for instance, would be worth around £40. Other names to look out for are E. & W. Anstie, W. A. & A. C. Churchman, Lambert & Butler and Ogden.

Postcards

Postcards were originally blank on one side with lines marked on the other to indicate where the address should be written. Picture postcards first made an appearance in around 1900 in Germany, a country that has always been at the forefront of new printing techniques. During the First World War, however, it was mostly the French and Belgian cards that ended up in Britain, when the troops used them to send messages back to their loved ones. The pictures on these postcards were typically sepia and sometimes hand-tinted (a process that was stopped eventually when it became evident that the people applying the colour were suffering from lead poisoning because they used to lick the tips of their brushes).

The British troops were particularly keen on the sexy postcards available abroad because the images were more explicit than anything they had ever seen before. At home they had had to make do with the saucy seaside variety created by artists like Donald McGill, with their big-busted, domineering females, skinny, henpecked husbands and a slightly *risqué double entendre* in the caption. McGill's vulgar cards were a familiar sight on every seaside prom from the early 1900s to the mid-1960s and are now well worth collecting.

It is said that France produced around 120 million erotic postcards every year during the First World War. For their wives or sweethearts, of course, most soldiers would choose something less provocative. Many of the more conventionally romantic cards were printed with sentimental verses and had silk panels with embroidered flowers. Unfortunately, there are so many of these around today that they currently have little commercial value.

As a general rule, anything dating from after the Second World War will be worth very little unless it is of special interest, maybe featuring early forms of transport, commemorating a famous disaster or showing a building or other landmark that no longer exists. Instalment cards are fun – whoever invented these knew a bit about marketing as each card showed only part of a picture and you needed 12, typically, to make up the complete image.

Autographs

Autograph-hunting is a cheap hobby and one day, if you have the patience to wait, it just might make you some money. The fun is that you never know at the time whose name is really going to become a legend. If you are serious about collecting autographs then you should try and get the celebrity to sign something relating to them, like an album cover or a concert or theatre programme. And don't forget that buyers will always be interested in other ephemera connected to the occasion, such as tickets, flyers, advertisements and reviews.

The demand for autographs has been increasing steadily over the years ever since the movie studios started sending out signed photographs of their film stars to the fans. Many of these young Hollywood hopefuls are long forgotten and their signatures are not worth much but those of such iconic figures as Charlie Chaplin, Laurel & Hardy and Mae West are now very collectable indeed.

Come the 1950s and 1960s and all of a sudden you have a new breed of showbiz celebrity – the pop star. Buddy Holly, Elvis Presley, Jimi Hendrix, John Lennon, to list but a few – if they died young then tragedy will add value to their names.

A vital factor in this field is authenticity and provenance. Celebrities don't always sign all their own photographs personally, especially those that their agents and fan clubs send out by the sackload. If you have a signed photograph you should have it checked by an expert and if the signature is a facsimile then forget it for it won't be worth the paper it is printed on.

Photographs are not the only artefacts to come with a signature, of course, and there is always a ready market for items of personal correspondence that bear a famous name. A letter that the English mathematician Sir Isaac Newton wrote to a friend fetched £13,000 at auction in 2003.

Old technology

Musical boxes

Mechanical musical boxes were first made in around 1850. The old ones are usually beautifully crafted in wood and decorated with marquetry inlay designed with musical motifs. The clockwork mechanism works by means of a metal 'comb' that consists of a number of sharp pins (tines) and a cylinder that has a number small protrusions or teeth. In the earliest models the cylinder and comb are exposed but these were later covered over with a sheet of glass as a safety measure. The cylinder rotates at a regular speed and the teeth pluck the tines in order to create the musical sound. Some musical boxes play just one tune but the large ones give you up to 12. In some more elaborate versions, bells or drums are incorporated to add accompaniment. These more elaborate musical boxes are worth more than the basic type, and some may go for several thousand pounds. Musical boxes are still produced today, often as jewellery cases.

Polyphones

The polyphone was invented in Germany in 1886, the pioneers being Paul Lochmann and Gustav Brachhausen, who also worked in partnership to manufacture and sell their invention. The polyphone was clearly inspired by the musical box and it works in a very similar way, though with a flat disc instead of a cylinder. One improvement was that it was easy to change these discs and so the choice of music was much greater.

Polyphones come in a variety of sizes. The largest is about 60 cm (24 inches) in diameter and up to 1.8 m (6 feet) tall and this type was designed for use in public places such as taverns. They are coin-operated and are in effect an early type of jukebox. If you would like one of these, in working order, be prepared to shell out anything up to £10,000. Failing that, you could settle for a smaller model that is more suitable for the home at around £400–800.

Phonographs

The American Thomas Edison discovered how to record sound in 1877. He displayed his phonograph or 'talking machine' to a rapturous audience, playing out a recording of his own voice reciting a line from the nursery rhyme 'Mary Had a Little Lamb'.

Edison's original phonograph consisted of a foil-covered cylinder, a stylus and an amplifying horn. It was operated by means of a manual crank handle at the side, which wound the clockwork mechanism that drove the cylinder. The machine was not sold commercially because the foil on the cylinder wore out very quickly. However, by 1886 Edison had developed the wax cylinder and phonographs went on sale to an enthusiastic public. Known as 'The Little Gem', there are still quite a few in circulation today, worth somewhere in the region of £400.

Gramophones

The lifespan of the phonograph was cut short by the gramophone, which was invented by another American, Emil Berliner, in 1887. Early versions, like the phonograph, were either small tabletop models or stand-alone

A British 'Monarch' gramophone with an oak horn

Cameras

The first practical method of photography was developed by Louis Daguerre in France in 1839 but it was the development of roll film in 1885 and George Eastman's small Kodak cameras that made it an affordable and easy pastime. Around 100,000 Americans bought one of Kodak's Box Brownies in 1901–02, its first year of production, and so began the era of the enthusiastic amateur. Before that, most people went to a professional photographer's studio to have their picture taken, and usually only for special occasions, such as marriage.

Kodak made slightly different versions of the Box Brownie for the English market (the Ensign) and Germany (the Ernemann) and followed this up with another popular model, the No 3 folding Pocket Camera, which stayed in production for around 15 years.

By the 1920s camera technology had developed considerably and the Germans proved to be the new pioneers with their superior Rolleiflex and Leica models. The Leica was the first camera to use 35mm film, the size most commonly used today. Japan entered the market at the end of the Second World War, with Nikon leading the field.

For true value, collectors tend to go for early models; a nineteenth-century mahogany studio camera mounted on a tripod with large folding bellows and hand-held flash-gun might set you back more than £1000, depending on the condition (it does not necessarily have to be fully operational) and overall appearance. At the other end of the scale you could pick up an early twentieth-century camera for as little as £30. It all depends on what it is. Most Japanese cameras are still modestly priced though some of the German Leicas and Rolleiflexes can fetch thousands of pounds.

cabinets, and they came with a manual crank handle and a large exposed brass horn. In later versions the horn was enclosed in the cabinet, with doors which for the first time offered a primitive form of volume control!

All types of gramophone are collectable and if you can find the right needles and records they can still be used. The picture of a little terrier called 'Nipper', looking into the horn of a gramophone, allegedly listening to the voice of his recently deceased master, will be familiar to anyone who has ever played one of the old 78s issued by HMV (His Master's Voice). Early models with the detachable horn are quite desirable – the horns used to get damaged so there are not so many of these around in good condition. You could be looking at £1000 or more here, whereas the later models with the built-in horns would be worth a lot less.

Lace, linens and samplers

Lace and linens

Machine-made lace first appeared in the late nineteenth century. It is easily identified because it is normally coarser than the real thing and the patterns are perfectly reproduced over and over. There is not much call for this today and the aficionado will only be interested in handmade lace, the older the better. The items that appear on the market nowadays are usually small pieces, such as collars, cuffs and flounces, and you may be surprised to learn that even when they are quite old and exquisitely worked, lace goods do not necessarily fetch enormously high prices. For example, you could find a late nineteenth-century Honiton lace collar for as little as £50.

Lace is often used as a trimming for household linens, such as tablecloths, napkins, sheets and pillowcases. Irish linen has long been considered the best quality in the world and it is worth looking out for. Only the best items will have any real value and they are difficult to find in pristine condition.

Samplers

It used to be fashionable for the daughters of wealthy families to spend their time producing a 'sample' that showed off their skills with a needle and thread in a single piece of work. There was no set pattern or design to these samplers but many of them featured the letters of the alphabet, the numbers 0–9, a house, flowers and trees, with a sentimental verse or an extract from a religious text in the centre. The more adventurous young needleworker would incorporate colourful pictures or designs that told a story – Adam and Eve in the Garden of Eden was a popular theme – and she would then add her name, her age (the average was eight to ten years) and the date she completed the piece. These individual personalized details are not only charming, they can also add value.

Parents often had these samplers framed and displayed them with pride as an early indication to potential suitors that their daughters were accomplished young ladies with all the makings of a good wife. Whether a sampler is framed or not does not necessarily affect its value but if it has been exposed to sunlight it is likely that the colours have faded and this is not desirable. On the other hand, samplers that have been rolled up – or even worse, folded – and stored for years may have been damaged by excessive damp, heat or moths. Condition certainly matters.

One thing that definitely influences the value of a sampler is the type of fabric and threads used: the finer the better. Real silks on linen are the best as these have always been expensive materials and they allow for much finer stitchwork than wool on a gauze backing.

A mid- to late-nineteenth-century sampler worked in silk on linen, in good condition, would fetch around £500 but you could pay three or four times as much for something older or more interesting than average, for instance an early example from America.

12

How to sell

Once you have separated your antiques and collectables from the junk it is time to decide how to turn them into hard cash. There are several routes open to you: car boot sale, antique dealer, auction, internet auction or private sale.

Which of these you choose will depend partly on what you want to sell. Car boot sales, antique shops and general auctions tend to attract speculative, impulsive customers – people who snap up something that happens to interest them on the spur of the moment. These places are fine for everyday bric-a-brac, but if you have something that you know is sought by collectors, then a well-advertised auction at a specialist saleroom is more likely to find buyers who will value the particular item you are trying to sell.

The growth of internet auctions in the last few years has enabled sellers to reach an even wider market around the world, cutting out the middleman. A collector in New Zealand who is missing volume five from his set of Victorian encyclopedias, for example, can now track down Mrs Smith in Yorkshire who just happens to be trying to sell that very book.

Car boot sales

Car boot sales are a popular way of selling off unwanted items – and they can be great fun too. Check the local press for details of car boot sales organized in your area and keep a close eye on the weather forecast – rain will not only put a damper on the proceedings, it could also damage your goods.

You don't need much in the way of gear to sell at a car boot sale but I would suggest the following:

- transport to get you and your stuff to the venue
- a collapsible table – something like a decorator's trestle table is ideal, unless you have a lot of heavy items
- a chair for each person
- cash float – you should take enough money to cover your stall rent (some organizers insist on cash up front) plus a few pounds' worth of small change
- a cash bag or money belt
- carrier bags, old newspapers and wrapping paper such as polystyrene or bubble-wrap
- refreshments
- loo roll

Good forward planning is the key to a successful day at a car boot sale. Make a list of everything you want to sell and decide in advance a) how much you are going to ask for each item and b) the lowest price you will be prepared to accept. You should also decide whether or not you are going to dispose of your things at give-away prices if need be or whether you will hold out, even if it means repacking and bringing everything home again. Before you venture out make sure you have done your research. Silly overpricing will put the punters off but serious underpricing could lose you a fortune. There's no harm in putting an optimistic price tag on each item, as long as it is within a reasonable range, but be prepared to haggle – it's part of the fun. Bargaining is quite an art and you need to be confident, so if you are feeling nervous or shy about this, take an extrovert friend to help you sell.

Antique dealers

The best way to find a good antique dealer is to ask your friends to recommend someone. If this doesn't work, then start calling in on your local antique shops and visiting the fairs that are held around the country every weekend. Talk to people and wait until you find someone you can trust.

If you have just a few portable items to sell you can take them straight to the dealer for a valuation. For bigger pieces, such as furniture, or maybe an entire house full of things, you should arrange for the dealer to call on you. If you are on your own, invite a friend or relative round at the same time for security and moral support.

A reputable dealer will not charge you for coming to your home but you should establish this beforehand just in case. Before the appointment, sort out exactly what it is you are putting up for sale so that there is no confusion on the day and make sure you have some idea in your own mind about how much you are willing to accept and whether you want to haggle. It is perfectly normal for a dealer to make an offer on the spot, pay up and take the goods away there and then, so be prepared for this. But don't be pressurized into selling if you are not happy with the price. You are entitled to get as many valuations as you like so just say you need more time before making your decision. If the dealer has been honest and really knows the local market you will probably find that all the others will come up with pretty much the same ballpark figure. In this case you may want to keep your goods instead of selling them or you may decide to find another way, such as an auction or the internet.

The pros:
- a dealer will pay you immediately, usually in cash
- your transaction will be a private arrangement between you and the dealer and you will not have to pay any commission to a third party
- the dealer will sort out and cover the cost of packing and transportation
- once you have sold an item the dealer has no comeback so the deal is entirely at their own risk

The cons:
- you will not get the top value for your goods because the dealer has to make a profit
- word gets around in the antiques business and as dealers are in competition with one another your private business may not end up being as private as you might have wished
- most dealers will 'cherry-pick', which means that they will offer to take the best but will leave the rest
- once you have sold an item the deal is done and there is no cooling-off period

Auctions

Some auction houses will sell anything and everything, including electrical goods and bric-a-brac. This can be very useful when clearing a house, as they will handle it all for you.

These auction houses usually set aside a particular day for selling ordinary household items and will keep this distinct from the days when they sell 'fine art'. Anything estimated at £50+ is probably worth putting into a 'fine art' auction. If you have a large collection of one particular type of thing, such as silver or toys, for example, try and find a specialist saleroom. It is probably best to avoid those places where they put antique and modern items through on the same day as serious buyers will tend to stay away – they won't want to waste their time watching old TVs and cookers going under the hammer.

If you think you may have something that is worth quite a lot, then maybe one of the big four houses will be the best choice. These are: Bonhams, Christie's, Phillips and Sotheby's.

Handy tips for choosing an auction house:

- visit a few local salerooms to see if they are handling the type of goods you want to sell
- make initial contact by telephone and ask what sort of goods they generally handle

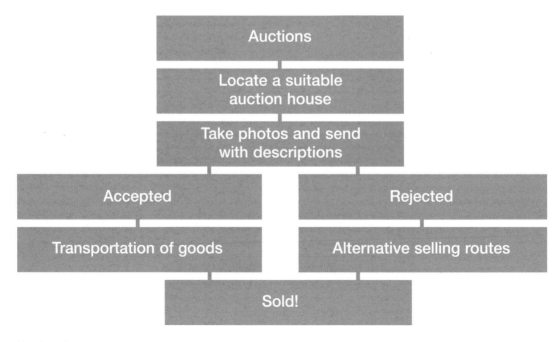

- most auctioneers want your business and may agree to handle goods that are really too good for their average sale and the customers they attract
- it is sometimes worth starting at the top as you have nothing to lose and if they don't want to handle your goods they will tell you soon enough

If your items are quite specialist, persevere in finding the right auction house, even if this means waiting several months. Some specialist auctions will not occur frequently but they are usually well advertised and well attended by dealers and collectors and so will give you your best chance of a good price.

Before making contact with an auction house make a list of all the items you have, together with a brief description of each. Make sure you've noted any identifying features, such as maker's marks, hallmarks or signatures, and be honest about any damage. Photograph everything individually, then send the pictures and the list to the auction house with a covering letter asking them if they would be interested in taking the matter further. This is better than turning up unannounced with all your stuff and expecting a valuer to appraise it on the spot without any prior warning.

If the auctioneers respond positively, you can arrange a home visit. There is not usually a charge for this but check first. The valuer will give an approximate price range for each item, or accumulation, that you might expect to achieve at auction. It is then up to you whether or not you want to go ahead. Remember that there are no guarantees that your goods will reach their estimated prices. On the other hand, you might be lucky and get much more than you expected on the day.

Transportation

If you have anything that is particularly heavy – or fragile – it's advisable to let the auction house arrange transportation. In most cases they will charge for this service but this should include proper insurance cover. If you are happy to take the goods yourself, make sure you pack everything carefully into strong boxes. You will probably have to get them to the auction quite some time before the sale.

Reserve prices

Auctions really are something of a gamble and if the bidding is not competitive your things could be knocked down for a fraction of their true worth. But there is a safety net available for you – the 'reserve'. By placing a reserve on your item you are setting a minimum selling price. This means that if it does not reach this price at auction your goods will be returned to you unsold. You may have to pay a handling or lotting fee. A good auctioneer will be able to advise you on setting realistic reserves.

Sales catalogues

All auctioneers issue a list of the lots they intend to auction on a particular day and some will go to the extra expense of producing an illustrated sales catalogue. It is up to them which items they choose for illustration and they will clearly be influenced by how valuable or unusual the pieces are. A good colour photograph will always catch the eye and the aim is to draw the bidders in. There's nothing to stop you from lobbying for your items to be featured in the auctioneer's catalogue but be prepared for a charge of around 10 per cent of the reserve price and come to a firm agreement beforehand.

Commission and fees

Most auctioneers work on commission calculated as a percentage of the selling price. This can vary – the average is 10 per cent but it can be as high as 20 per cent – so it is important to establish exactly what the commission will be before putting anything into the sale. It is in the auctioneer's interest to make sure your goods are advertised appropriately and placed in the most suitable auction as the higher the selling price the greater their commission. If your goods fail to sell for whatever reason you may be charged for transporting them back to you plus a small handling fee.

In most cases you will be charged VAT on the commission plus around 1 per cent of the 'hammer price' for insurance. So let's say your items were knocked down at £150 (hammer price). You would receive £130.87 and the deductions would add up as follows:

Auctioneer's commission @ 10%:	£15.00
VAT @ 17.5% (on the commission):	£2.63
1% insurance (on the hammer price):	£1.50
Total deductions:	£19.13

You can see from all this that selling at auction can be quite a lengthy process from first contact to final sale and even then you will probably have to wait a few more days for your cheque from the auction house. On the plus side, what could be more exciting than watching two bidders slugging it out to buy something that you once owned at a price you could never have dreamed of.

The internet

There are two ways of selling goods over the internet: to a private collector or in an internet auction.

Private collectors

If you have items that are likely to appeal to specialist collectors you may be able to contact them directly and arrange a deal between yourselves. This can provide excellent value for both parties because there is no third party involved. But you need to be sure how much your item is worth so do your research first.

Internet auctions

Internet auctions have rapidly become an extremely popular and efficient way of dealing in antiques and collectables as it puts buyers and sellers from all over the world in touch who would never have had the opportunity to find each other before. You don't need any specialized computer knowledge but you will need unrestricted access to the internet and to be reasonably comfortable using it. There are a number of auction sites, all operating on similar principles, including: Ebay, Ebay UK, Auctions UK and Whybidmore Collectibles. Log on to their sites and study their terms and conditions before you start. Most reputable sites place a restriction on what you can offer for sale, banning weapons, for example.

It is best to stick to things that are easy to post or ship, though you can specify that the buyer should be responsible for collection and insurance. In this case an estimate of the likely cost involved will help bidders to decide their maximum bid.

The customer will probably locate your goods from searches within the site so stick to simple and common descriptions. A well-known maker or designer will also be easy to find. For example, a Wedgwood teapot would attract collectors of Wedgwood and collectors of teapots.

How to sell

Before deciding on an auction site, you need to decide whether your goods are suitable for sale worldwide or just in your own country. Although advertising worldwide gives you access to many more buyers, the cost of shipping large items abroad may deter foreign bidders.

To register with an auction site you will have to complete an electronic application form, which will be quite lengthy and may ask for your credit card and bank details. You may find it easier if you print off the form and do a dummy run before filling it in for real on-line.

Before placing your item on the site, you need to prepare a detailed description, including dimensions, full details of any marks and any damage. Be as accurate as possible and don't exaggerate. Avoid using words or phrases such as 'perfect' or 'original condition' lightly. Buyers on the internet have broadly the same consumer rights as anyone else so it is advisable to err on the conservative side in your descriptions. A photo of the piece is important as a lot of buyers will be put off if there is no picture to go with the description.

You will need to fill in a form to register the item you are putting up for sale and again it is advisable to print it first and practise filling it in so that you don't make any mistakes. You will generally have various options, such as the length of time you will allow bids to come in before you agree a sale (this is usually three, five or seven days) and you can set the bidding increments, say £1 for low value goods or £5 for more valuable pieces. Establish whether you are including the cost of postage or shipping in the reserve price or alternatively specify this within the general description. You also need to decide on the method of payment – cheque, postal order, credit card, etc. Be prepared to deal in US dollars if you are using an American or international auction site.

In order to work out the cost of sending your piece to the successful bidder you will need to know how much it weighs – don't forget to add the weight of the packaging. When you know what the overall weight will be, check on the best method of delivery with the post office or shipper. Remember that registered or recorded delivery is much more expensive than ordinary post and you will need to factor this in. Finally, check that the compensation they offer for loss or damage is adequate.

After the auction

Although the auction will run itself, it is important to check your email messages every day as potential customers could be contacting you with queries. As soon as the deadline has passed the auction site will email you with details of who has bought your item and for how much. It is then up to you to sort everything out with your buyer. From now on there has to be an element of trust: your buyer has to trust that you have been honest in your description of the item and that you will deliver it safely. You have to trust that you will get paid. It may seem that you are risking a lot but many of these internet auction sites are now well established and so they have demonstrated that they work. They clearly fulfil a need and most deals are hassle-free.

As an extra safeguard the sites have a feedback board and this is where buyers and sellers can post information, both good and bad, about their dealings. If someone has been ripped off then everyone will soon know about it and the people running the auction site will do their best to make sure that the swindlers cannot get away with it again. So check out the feedback board before you start.

In most cases you will be charged a set lotting fee for each lot (which can consist of more than one item). This is usually quite low but is payable even if your lot does not sell. In addition, internet auction sites take a commission on every sale, just like any other auctioneer, and the rates vary but can be as low as one per cent of the selling price. They will take their commission from your credit card but will inform you by email beforehand.

Further reading

General antiques books

Miller's Antiques Price Guide, Ed. Elizabeth Norfolk (Miller's Publications, annually)

Miller's Collectibles Price Guide, Ed. Madeleine Marsh (Miller's Publications, annually)

Miller's Antiques Shops, Fairs & Auctions in the UK and Eire (Miller's Publications, annually)

Antique Dealer's Guide, Tony Curtis (Lyle Publications, 2002)

Pictures

Miller's Price Guide: Pictures, Ed. Hugh St Clair (Miller's Publications, annually)

Victorian Painters (*Dictionary of British Art*, Vol. IV), Christopher Wood (Antique Collectors' Club, 1995)

Victorian Painting ('World of Art' series), Julian Treuherz (Thames and Hudson, 1993)

Dictionary of British Artists 1880–1940 (*Dictionary of British Art*, Vol. IV, Antique Collectors' Club, 1995)

Lawrence's Dealer Print Prices International 2002 (Dealers Choice Books, 2002)

Buying and Selling Pictures Successfully, Alan G. Thompson (Robert Hale, 1997)

Furniture

Buyer's Guide to British Furniture Craftsmen, Eds. Melvyn Stuart Earle and Marie Earle (Craftsman Publishing Co, 1993)

British Antique Furniture: Price Guide and Reasons for Value 2004, John Andrews (Antique Collectors' Club, 2004)

Repairing and Restoring Antique Furniture, John Rodd (David & Charles, 1995)

Modern Furniture Classics: Postwar to Post-modernism, Charlotte and Peter Fiell (Thames and Hudson, 2001)

Furniture: a Concise History ('World of Art' series), Edward Lucie-Smith (Thames and Hudson, 1979)

Sotheby's Concise Encyclopedia of Furniture (Conran Octopus, 1994)

English Furniture Styles, 1500–1830, Ralph Fastnedge (Penguin, 1969)

Art Deco Furniture: The French Designers, Alastair Duncan (Thames and Hudson, 1997)

Regency Furniture, Frances Collard (Antique Collectors' Club, 1985)

British Furniture, 1880–1915, Pauline Agius (Antique Collectors' Club, 1978)

Pictorial Dictionary of British 18th Century Furniture Design: The Printed Sources, Ed. Elizabeth White (Antique Collectors' Club, 1992)

Pictorial Dictionary of British 19th Century Furniture Design (Antique Collectors' Club, 1976)

Pottery and porcelain

New Handbook of British Pottery and Porcelain Marks, Geoffrey A. Godden (Ebury Press, 1999)

Sotheby's Concise Encyclopedia of Porcelain, Ed. David Battie (Little, Brown & Co, 1990)

The Beswick Price Guide, May Harvey (Francis Joseph, 1997)

Collecting Rhead Pottery, Bernard Bumpus (Francis Joseph, 1999)

The Complete Clarice Cliff, Howard and Pat Watson (Francis Joseph, 2003)

The Lyle Price Guide to Doulton, Mick Yewman (Lyle Publications, 1986)

Lyle Doulton Price Guide, Tony Curtis (Lyle Publications, 1998)

Moorcroft: A Guide to Moorcroft Pottery 1897–1903, Paul Atterbury and Beatrice Moorcroft (Richard Dennis Publications, 1993)

Collecting Moorcroft Pottery: Colour Price Guide, Robert Walker-Prescott (Francis Joseph, 2002)

The Pendelfin Collectors Handbook, Stella M. Ashbrook and Frank Salmon (Francis Joseph, 1999)

Worcester Porcelain in the Marshall Collection,
   Dinah Reynolds (Ashmolean Museum
   Publications, 1988)
The Dictionary of Worcester Porcelain 1751–1851,
   John Sandon (Antique Collectors' Club, 2002)
Spode and Copeland Marks, Robert Copeland
   (Cassell Illustrated, 1993)
Spode Transfer Printed Ware 1784–1833, David
   Drakard and Paul Holdway (Antique Collectors'
   Club, 2002)
*Miller's Collector's Guide: Staffordshire Figures of
   the 19th & 20th Centuries*, Kit Harding (Miller's
   Publications, 2000)
Price Guide to Wade, Stella M. Ashbrook (Francis
   Joseph, 2003)

Glass
*Collector's Companion to Carnival Glass:
   Identification and Values*, Bill Edwards and Mike
   Carwile (Collector Books, 2003)
*Standard Encyclopedia of Carnival Glass Price
   Guide*, Bill Edwards and Mike Carwile (Collector
   Books, 2002)
Miller's How to Compare and Value Art Glass,
   Louise Luther (Miller's Publications, 2002)
*Miller's Collector's Guide: Popular Glass of 19th
   & 20th Centuries*, Raymond Notley (Miller's
   Publications, 2000)
Lalique, Tony L. Mortimer (Book Sales, 1988)

Metalware
The Price Guide to Antique Silver, Peter Waldron
   (Antique Collectors' Club, 2001)
English Silver Hallmarks ('Dealer Guides' series),
   Stanley W. Fisher (Foulsham, 1992)
*EPNS: Electroplated Nickel Silver & Old Sheffield
   Plate Makers' Marks 1858–1943* ('Dealer Guides'
   series), George Mappin (Foulsham, 1992)
*Yesterday's Silver for Today's Table: A Silver
   Collector's Guide to Elegant Dining*, Richard
   Osterberg (Schiffer Publishing, 2001)
*Antique Brass & Copper: Identification & Value
   Guide*, Mary Frank Gaston (Collector Books,
   1991)

*Metalwares Price Guide: Including Silver, Brass,
   Copper, Pewter and More*, Marilyn E. Dragowick
   (Krause Publications, n.d.)
Collecting Antique Copper and Brass, Peter
   Hornsby (Moorland, 1989)
Brass and Brassware, David J. Eveleigh (Shire
   Publications, 1999)

Clocks and watches
*The Watch and Clockmakers' Handbook,
   Dictionary and Guide*, F. J. Britten (Antique
   Collectors' Club, 1993)
Encyclopedia of Antique American Clocks, Robert
   W. and Harriet Swedberg (Krause Publications,
   2001)
*Gustav Becker Clocks, A Guide to Identification
   & Prices*, Tran D. Ly (U.S. Books, 1997)
Antique Trader Price Guide: Clocks, Eds. Kyle
   Husfloen and Mark Moran (Krause Publications,
   2003)
Miller's Buyer's Guide: Clocks & Barometers,
   Derek Roberts (Miller's Publications, 2002)
French Bronze Clocks, Elke Niehüser (Schiffer
   Publishing, 1999)
Repairing Antique Clocks, Eric P. Smith (David &
   Charles, 2002)
Breitling Timepieces: 1884 to the Present, Benno
   Richter (Schiffer Publishing, 2000)
Finding and Restoring Longcase Clocks, Anthony
   Ells (The Crowood Press, 2001)
Watchmakers & Clockmakers of the World, Brian
   Loomes (N. A. G. Press, 1993)
Longcase Clocks, Joanna Greenlaw (Shire
   Publications, 1999)
Collectable Clocks 1880–1940, Alan and Rita
   Shenton (Antique Collectors' Club, 1995)
*100 Years of Vintage Watches, A Collector's
   Identification & Price Guide*, Dean Judy (Krause
   Publications, 2002)
Miller's Collector's Guide: Watches, Frankie Liebe
   (Miller's Publications, 1999)
Miller's How to Compare and Value Wristwatches,
   Jonathan Scatchard (Mitchell Beazley,
   2004)

Complete Price Guide to Watches, Cookey
   Shugart (Collector Books, 2003)
Watches International, Caroline Childers (Rizzoli
   International Publications, 2002)
Collecting & Repairing Watches, Max Cutmore
   (David & Charles, 2001)
Collectible Wristwatches, René Pannier (Éditions
   Flammarion, 2001)
Wristwatch Annual, Peter Braun (Abbeville Press,
   annually)
The Pocket Watch Handbook, M. Cutmore (David
   & Charles, 2002)

Jewellery

*Vintage Jewelry 1920–1940s: A Price and
   Identification Guide*, Leigh Leshner (Krause
   Publications, 2002)
Official Price Guide to Costume Jewelry,
   Harrice Simons Miller (House of Collectibles,
   2002)
Complete Price Guide to Antique Jewelry, Richard
   E. Gilbert and James H. Wolf (Independent
   Publishers Group, 2000)
Miller's Antiques Checklist: Jewellery, Stephen
   Giles (Miller's Publications, 1997)
Antique Jewelry with Prices, Doris J. Snell (Krause
   Publications, 1997)

Medals, coins and stamps

*Standard Catalog of World Coins: World Coin
   Listings by Date and Mint*, Chester L. Krause,
   Clifford Mishler and Colin R. Bruce II (Krause
   Publications, 2001)

*Coincraft's Standard Catalogue of English and UK
   Coins: 1066 to Date*, Richard Lobel (Coincraft,
   1999)
Collecting Military Medals: A Beginner's Guide,
   Colin Narbeth (Lutterworth Press, 2002)
Military Badge Collecting, John Gaylor and Ray
   Westlake (Pen & Sword Books, 2002)
Stanley Gibbons Stamp Catalogue (several
   volumes, Stanley Gibbons Ltd)

Toys

Miller's Antiques Checklist: Toys & Games, Hugo
   Marsh (Miller's Publications, 1995)
*Linda Mullins' Teddy Bears & Friends: Identification
   & Price Guide* (Hobby House Press, 2000)
*Schroeders Collectable Toys: Antique to Modern
   Price Guide*, Sharon Huxford and Bob Huxford
   (Collector Books, 2001)
*Miller's Teddy Bears: A Complete Collector's
   Guide*, Sue Pearson (Miller's Publications, 2001)
Christie's Century of Teddy Bears, Leyla Maniera
   (Watson-Guptill Publications, 2001)
Steiff Identification & Price Guide, Linda Mullins
   (Hobby House Press, 2001)
The Space Toy Price Guide, Frank Thompson
   (A. & C. Black, 1995)
200 Years of Dolls: Identification and Price Guide,
   Dawn Herlocher (Antique Trader Books, 1996)

Books

The Official Price Guide to Collecting Books,
   Marie Tedford and Pat Goudey (House of
   Collectibles, 2002)

Clubs, fairs and websites

General antiques websites

www.invaluable.com
www.antiques-online.uk.com
www.antiqueweb.com
www.collectingnetwork.com
www.atg-online.com (Antiques Trade Gazette)

Antiques fairs

www.antiques-atlas.com

British collectors' clubs

www.antiquesworld.co.uk/Clubs/clubs_aznom

Furniture

The Furniture History Society,
1 Mercedes Cottages, St John's Road,
Haywards Heath, West Sussex RH16 6EH

Pottery and porcelain collectors' clubs

Pen Delfin Family Circle, Nancy Falkenham, 1250
Terwillegar Avenue, Oshawa, Ontario L1J 7A5,
Canada

Bunnykins Collectors' Club, 6 Beckett Way
Lewes, East Sussex BN7 2EB
www.bunnykins.collectorsclub@btinternet.co.uk

The Clarice Cliff Collectors' Club, Fantasque House,
Tennis Drive, The Park, Nottingham NG7 1AE
www.claricecliff.com

Moorcroft Collectors' Club, W. Moorcroft plc,
Sandbach Road, Burslem, Stoke-on-Trent,
Staffordshire ST6 2DQ
Tel. 01782 214345
club@moorcroft.com www.moorcroft.com

Royal Doulton International Collectors' Club,
Sir Henry Doulton House, Forge Lane, Etruria,
Stoke on Trent, Staffordshire ST1 5NN
www.royal-doulton.com/main/level_one/collectors

The Official International Wade Collectors' Club,
Wade Ceramics Limited, Royal Works,
Westport Road, Burslem, Stoke-on-Trent ST6 4AP
Tel. 01782 577321
www.wade.co.uk

Glassware

Carnival Glass Society UK Ltd.,
PO Box 14, Hayes, Middlesex UB3 5NU

Specialist Glass Fairs Ltd, 155 St John's Road,
Congleton, Cheshire CW12 2EH
www.glassfairs.co.uk

Clocks and watches

British Watch & Clock Collectors' Association,
5 Cathedral Lane, Truro, Cornwall TR1 2SQ
Tel. 01872 41953

Medals, coins and stamps

Military Historical Society, Lt. Col. Robin Hodges,
Secretary, National Army Museum, Royal Hospital
Road, London SW3 4HT

Order and Medals Research Society,
PO Box 1904, Southam CV47 2ZX
www.orms.org.uk

www.britishmilitarymedals.co.uk

The British Association of Numismatic Societies,
Mr P. Mernick, Secretary BANS, c/o General
Services, 42 Campbell Road, London E3 4DT
Tel. 020 8980 5672
www.coinclubs.freeserve.co.uk

Toys

Corgi Collectors' Club,
c/o Corgi Classics Limited, Meridian East,
Meridian Business Park, Leicester LE3 2RL
www.corgi.co.uk

The Hornby Railway Collectors' Association,
PO Box 3443, Yeovil, Somerset BA21 4XR
Tel. 01935 474830
www.hrca.net

Hugglets Teddy Bear Club,
PO Box 290, Brighton, East Sussex BN2 1DR
Tel. 01273 697974
www.hugglets.co.uk

Matchbox Toys International Collectors' Association,
PO Box 120, Deeside, Flintshire CH5 3HE
Tel. 01244 539414
www.matchboxclub.com

Merrythought International Collectors' Club,
Ironbridge, Telford, Shropshire TF8 7NJ
Tel. 01952 433116
www.merrythought.co.uk/icc/icc.asp

Muffin the Mule Collectors' Club, 12 Woodland
Close, Woodford Green, Essex IG8 0QH
www.muffin-the-mule.com

Russian Doll Collectors' Club, Gardeners Cottage
Hatchlands, East Clandon, Surrey GU4 7RT
Tel. 01483 222789
www.russiandolls.co.uk

Train Collectors' Society,
PO Box 20340, London NW11 6ZE
www.traincs.demon.co.uk

Musical boxes

Musical Box Society of Great Britain,
PO Box 299, Waterbeach, Cambridgeshire
CB4 8DT
www.mbsgb.org.uk

Postcards and autographs

The Post Card Club of Great Britain,
34 Harper House, St James's Crescent,
London SW9 7LW

Autograph Club of Great Britain, 47 Web
Crescent, Dawley, Telford, Shropshire TF4 3DS
www.acogb.com

Quiz answers

Thirty questions (page 17): 1c; 2b; 3a; 4a; 5c;
6a; 7b; 8b; 9a; 10a; 11a; 12a; 13a; 14b; 15c;
16c; 17a; 18c; 19a; 20c; 21a; 22b; 23b; 24c;
25a; 26c; 27a; 28a; 29b; 30a

Kite mark quiz (page 36): 1=1844; 2=1845;
3=1843; 4=1870; 5=1875; 6=1890–1895;
7=1900–1905

Wade piggy bank quiz (page 40): baby=a;
sister=b; brother=b; mother=c; father=a

Hallmarks quiz (page 62): 1 Edinburgh 1898;
2 Birmingham 1905; 3 Sheffield 1897; 4 London
1907; 5 Sheffield 1902; 6 London 1897;
7 Birmingham 1909; 8 Edinburgh 1897

Birthstone test (page 95): January, garnet, red,
constancy; February, amethyst, purple, sincerity;
March, bloodstone or aquamarine, green or red or
blue, courage; April, diamond, white or clear, inno-
cence; May, emerald, green, love and success; June,
pearl or moonstone or alexandrite, cream, health
and longevity; July, ruby, red, contentment; August,
sardonyx or peridot, light green, married happiness;
September, sapphire, blue, clear thinking; October,
opal or tourmaline, multi-coloured, hope; November,
topaz, orange or brown, fidelity; December,
turquoise or lapis lazuli, blueish-green, prosperity

Index

Page numbers in *italics* refer to illustrations

Filming *Cash in the Attic* on location. *From left to right:* Troy Hermer, Paul Hayes, Graham Kelly, Alistair Appleton, Caroline Coombs and Gill Waddington

Acknowledgements

Many people have contributed indirectly, but vitally, to this book. The first 'thank you' goes to my dad, Peter Hayes, who, together with his legion of friends in the trade, introduced me to the magical world of antiques. I am also massively grateful to everyone who helped to get me 'on the box', so special thanks to Mel Eriksen, the producer who 'discovered' me, to James Burstall of Leopard Films, who signed me up for *Cash in the Attic*, and to everyone at Limelight. From the television programme, Alistair, Lorne, Jonty and the entire production team led by Bernard and Mike – all of them true professionals who just happen to be great fun to work with, as indeed was each and every contestant on the show.

At the sharp end of actually writing this book I had great help from my family. First thanks go to my wife, Kathryn, who worked with me throughout, marshalling my random outpourings and somehow transferring them to paper in logical sequence. Between both of us having day jobs, and the presence of three boisterous boys in the house, none of this help would have been possible without the perpetually available assistance of star grandmas, Eileen and Muriel.

Lastly, thanks to Derek Hollinrake, whose helpful comments and suggestions very much influenced the final shape of this book.